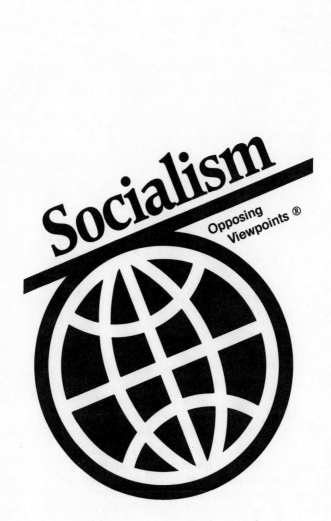

Socialism

Opposing Viewpoints ®

Other Volumes Available in the *ISMS SERIES:*

Capitalism
Communism
Feminism
Internationalism
Nationalism
Racism

BRUNO LEONE received his B.A. (Phi Kappa Phi) from Arizona State University and his M.A. in history from the University of Minnesota. A Woodrow Wilson Fellow (1967) and former instructor at Minneapolis Community College, he has taught history, anthropology, and political science. In 1974-75, he was awarded a Fellowship by the National Endowment for the Humanities to research the intellectual origins of American Democracy. He has edited numerous titles in the *Opposing Viewpoints Series.*

The Isms: Modern Doctrines and Movements

Socialism

Opposing Viewpoints ®

REVISED EDITION

Bruno Leone

91-1953

Greenhaven Press

577 Shoreview Park Road
St. Paul, Minnesota 55126

Library of Congress Cataloging-in-Publication Data

Socialism : opposing viewpoints.

(The Isms)
Includes bibliographies and index.
1. Socialism. 2. Utopian socialism. 3. Public welfare. I. Leone, Bruno, 1939-   . II. Series.
HX72.S63   1986   335   86-335
ISBN 0-89908-386-2 (lib. bdg.)
ISBN 0-89908-361-7 (pbk.)

Second Edition
Revised

"Congress shall make no law...
abridging the freedom of speech,
or of the press."

first amendment to the U.S. Constitution

The basic foundation of our democracy is the first amendment guarantee of freedom of expression. The Opposing Viewpoints books are dedicated to the concept of this basic freedom and the idea that it is more important to practice it than to enshrine it.

Contents

Chapter 3: Socialism and Welfare

Chapter 4: Socialism Today

Why Consider Opposing Viewpoints?

"It is better to debate a question without settling it than to settle a question without debating it."

Joseph Joubert (1754-1824)

The Importance of Examining Opposing Viewpoints

The purpose of the Opposing Viewpoints books, and this book in particular, is to present balanced, and often difficult to find, opposing points of view on complex and sensitive issues.

Probably the best way to become informed is to analyze the positions of those who are regarded as experts and well studied on issues. It is important to consider every variety of opinion in an attempt to determine the truth. Opinions from the mainstream of society should be examined. But also important are opinions that are considered radical, reactionary, or minority as well as those stigmatized by some other uncomplimentary label. An important lesson of history is the eventual acceptance of many unpopular and even despised opinions. The ideas of Socrates, Jesus, and Galileo are good examples of this.

Readers will approach this book with their own opinions on the issues debated within it. However, to have a good grasp of one's own viewpoint, it is necessary to understand the arguments of those with whom one disagrees. It can be said that those who do not completely understand their adversary's point of view do not fully understand their own.

A persuasive case for considering opposing viewpoints has been presented by John Stuart Mill in his work *On Liberty*. When examining controversial issues it may be helpful to reflect on this suggestion:

> The only way in which a human being can make some approach to knowing the whole of a subject, is by hearing what can be said about it by persons of every variety of opinion, and studying all modes in which it can be looked at by every character of mind. No wise man ever acquired his wisdom in any mode but this.

Analyzing Sources of Information

The Opposing Viewpoints books include diverse materials taken from magazines, journals, books, and newspapers, as well as statements and position papers from a wide range of individuals, organizations and governments. This broad spectrum of sources helps to develop patterns of thinking which are open to the consideration of a variety of opinions.

Pitfalls to Avoid

A pitfall to avoid in considering opposing points of view is that of regarding one's own opinion as being common sense and the most rational stance and the point of view of others as being only opinion and naturally wrong. It may be that another's opinion is correct and one's own is in error.

Another pitfall to avoid is that of closing one's mind to the opinions of those with whom one disagrees. The best way to approach a dialogue is to make one's primary purpose that of understanding the mind and arguments of the other person and not that of enlightening him or her with one's own solutions. More can be learned by listening than speaking.

It is my hope that after reading this book the reader will have a deeper understanding of the issues debated and will appreciate the complexity of even seemingly simple issues on which good and honest people disagree. This awareness is particularly important in a democratic society such as ours where people enter into public debate to determine the common good. Those with whom one disagrees should not necessarily be regarded as enemies, but perhaps simply as people who suggest different paths to a common goal.

Developing Basic Reading and Thinking Skills

In this book carefully edited opposing viewpoints are purposely placed back to back to create a running debate; each viewpoint is preceded by a short quotation that best expresses the author's main argument. This format instantly plunges the reader into the midst of a controversial issue and greatly aids that reader in mastering the basic skill of recognizing an author's point of view.

A number of basic skills for critical thinking are practiced in the activities that appear throughout the books in the series. Some of the skills are:

Evaluating Sources of Information The ability to choose from among alternative sources the most reliable and accurate source in relation to a given subject.

Separating Fact from Opinion The ability to make the basic distinction between factual statements (those that can be demonstrated or verified empirically) and statements of opinion (those that are beliefs or attitudes that cannot be proved).

Identifying Stereotypes The ability to identify oversimplified, exaggerated descriptions (favorable or unfavorable) about people and insulting statements about racial, religious or national groups, based upon misinformation or lack of information.

Recognizing Ethnocentrism The ability to recognize attitudes or opinions that express the view that one's own race, culture, or group is inherently superior, or those attitudes that judge another culture or group in terms of one's own.

It is important to consider opposing viewpoints and equally important to be able to critically analyze those viewpoints. The activities in this book are designed to help the reader master these thinking skills. Statements are taken from the book's viewpoints and the reader is asked to analyze them. This technique aids the reader in developing skills that not only can be applied to the viewpoints in this book, but also to situations where opinionated spokespersons comment on controversial issues. Although the activities are helpful to the solitary reader, they are most useful when the reader can benefit from the interaction of group discussion.

Using this book and others in the series should help readers develop basic reading and thinking skills. These skills should improve the readers' ability to understand what they read. Readers should be better able to separate fact from opinion, substance from rhetoric and become better consumers of information in our media-centered culture.

This volume of the Opposing Viewpoints books does not advocate a particular point of view. Quite the contrary! The very nature of the book leaves it to the reader to formulate the opinions he or she finds most suitable. My purpose as publisher is to see that this is made possible by offering a wide range of viewpoints which are fairly presented.

David L. Bender
Publisher

Preface to First Edition

In the early nineteenth century, Robert Owen, a native of Wales, became part-owner of a mill in New Lanark, Scotland. Unlike the vast majority of industrialists of his day, Owen's chief concern was people, not profits. Accordingly, he devoted himself to the betterment of the working and living standards of his employees. He converted New Lanark into a model factory town, establishing cooperative stores, democratic town meetings, and a host of other reforms unheard of at the time. In 1827, a sympathetic English periodical called *Co-operative Magazine*, used the term "socialism" to label Owen's experiment at New Lanark. Many historians and political scientists agree that this was probably the first time the term socialism appeared in print to describe a particular view of an ideal human society.

Certainly, Owen was not history's first socialist. As early as the eighteenth century, especially in France, there were numerous individuals crying for societal reforms along lines similar to Owen's. Primarily concerned with the economic deprivation of the lower classes, Claude Henri Saint-Simon, "Gracchus" Babeuf, Charles Fourier, and others, stressed the need for a fairer distribution of wealth. Most of their schemes involved a radical reorganization of the economic and social structure of society. Although none of these men lived to see their ideas bear fruit, they established themselves as the forerunners of the modern socialist movement.

Modern socialism arose in the nineteenth century as a reaction to capitalism, the economic system which became dominant in Western Europe during the Industrial Revolution. The rise of capitalism was characterized by a growing concentration of wealth in the hands of the owners of industry. For the most part, this wealth was being generated by a large army of ill-paid, overworked, and powerless laborers. Although more than a century of labor organizing and governmental regulation in the industrialized democracies of the world have managed to remove most of the excesses which accompanied rising capitalism, socialism has lost little of its early momentum. Indeed, socialists still vigorously contend that the persistent imbalance in wealth between upper and lower classes fully justifies their movement.

Both early and contemporary socialists agree upon two basic points. First, they argue that the existing capitalistic order is unfair and heavily weighed against the working class. Second, they are convinced that a more equitable system can be developed. This latter point, namely, that society *can* restructure its economic institutions along just and morally sound lines so as to insure fairness to all, is socialism's essential driving force.

By definition, socialism is a doctrine that advocates public ownership and operation of the means of production and distribution of goods and services in a nation. One of the most authoritative statements explaining the principles of socialism was formulated in 1951 at a meeting of the Socialist International in Germany. It reads in part:

> "Socialism seeks to replace capitalism by a system in which the public interest takes precedence over the interest of private profit. The immediate economic aims of socialist policy are full employment, higher production, a rising standard of life, social security and a fair distribution of incomes and property.
>
> "In order to achieve these ends, production must be planned in the interest of the people as a whole.
>
> "Such planning is incompatible with the concentration of economic power in the hands of a few. It requires effective democratic control of the economy."

The allure of socialism cannot be denied, even by its severest critics. Concepts such as economic equality, social justice, and political democracy appeal to the highest moral instincts of humanity, while the promise of full employment, rising living standards, and complete financial security serve to fulfill basic human needs. Yet ironically, the realization of a workable socialist order is questionable. Not only must dedicated socialists contend with the formidable opposition of equally dedicated capitalists, they must also deal with dissension within their own ranks. In fact, one of the most frustrating problems socialists have continually faced is disagreement among themselves as to their immediate and long-range goals and the methods necessary to achieve them.

This volume of opposing viewpoints attempts to acquaint the reader with the meaning of socialism and the evolution of socialist thought. The viewpoints include the ideas of some of the major socialist thinkers of the last and present centuries. In order to illustrate the depth and continual nature of the controversy induced by the arrival of socialism on the world scene, the critical viewpoints are drawn both from within and outside of the socialist movement.

Preface to Second Edition

It is with pleasure and an enormous degree of satisfaction that the second edition of Greenhaven Press's *ISMS Series: Opposing Viewpoints* has been published. The Series was so well received when it initially was made available in 1978 that plans for its revision were almost immediately formulated. During the following years, the enthusiasm of librarians and classroom teachers provided the editor with the necessary encouragement to complete the project.

While the Opposing Viewpoints format of the series has remained the same, each of the books has undergone a major revision. Because the series is developed along historical lines, materials were added or deleted in the opening chapters only where historical interpretations have changed or new sources were uncovered. The final chapters of each book have been comprehensively recast to reflect changes in the national and international situations since the original titles were published.

The Series began with six titles: *Capitalism, Communism, Internationalism, Nationalism, Racism,* and *Socialism.* A new and long overdue title, *Feminism,* has been added and several additional ones are being considered for the future. The editor offers his deepest gratitude to the dedicated and talented editorial staff of Greenhaven Press for its countless and invaluable contributions. A special thanks goes to Bonnie Szumski, whose gentle encouragement and indomitable aplomb helped carry the developing manuscripts over many inevitable obstacles. Finally, the editor thanks all future readers and hopes that the 1986 edition of the *ISMS Series* will enjoy the same reception as its predecessor.

Utopian Socialism

Introduction

The earliest school of socialist thought is usually referred to as utopian socialism. Led by Charles Fourier and Claude Saint-Simon in France, Robert Owen in England, and Horace Greeley and Charles Dana in the United States, the utopian socialists had visionary notions of what human society should be like. Many believed that it was possible to organize ideal communities of pre-arranged size. These communities would be composed of a numerically balanced cross-section of people including farmers, industrial workers, artists, and, in some cases, capitalists. They would be stable and self-sustaining, insuring all communal members of a continual and adequate livelihood. Although there would not be absolute economic equality, certain "safeguards" would insure that the differences in wealth would not be as excessive as in a purely capitalistic society.

The ideas of the utopian socialists were predicated upon certain moral laws they believed to be an inherent part of human nature. (Societal peace and harmony, and mutual help, were preeminent among these "laws.") Most felt that the advance of civilization was largely responsible for corrupting humankind and obsuring that which was a natural part of it. If man was properly educated and made aware of what his relationship to his fellow man should be, the utopian socialists assumed that their schemes might be readily adopted. Several utopian communities were, in fact, organized, the most famous being Robert Owen's New Harmony on the banks of the Wabash River in Indiana. None, however, succeeded.

The failure of utopian socialism can be attributed to the movement's lack of understanding of several primary changes occurring in modern European society. The rapid growth of industry and the attending rise of capitalism were events of revolutionary significance. Europe was on the move and in its wake remained the foundations of a totally new socioeconomic order. The newly emergent capitalist class was rapidly accumulating great wealth and building such a broad base of political power that it was little disposed to tolerate communal pipedreams. The workers, for their part, were in too depressed and uneducated a state to fully appreciate and be seduced by those same dreams.

The socialist who grasped the revolutionary nature of the times was Karl Marx. Rejecting utopian socialism in favor of what he termed "scientific socialism," Marx claimed that by and large, changes in the economic structure of society were the result of class conflict. In his painstakingly researched work, *Das Kapital* *(Capital)*, he threaded through the whole of recorded history to document his theory. He concluded that if any meaningful change was to be successfully achieved, it would have to follow a conflict between the two principle classes of his day, the capitalists and the workers (or, as he called them, bourgeoisie and proletarians). In other words, Marx was not seeking natural or moral laws for guidance; he was turning to the lessons of history. (Although he was associated with the Communist party of his day, Marx considered himself a "scientific socialist." For the distinction between socialism and communism, see *Communism* in the *ISMS Series.*)

The following viewpoints present the ideas of some of the most prominent and influential of the utopian socialists. The viewpoint by Karl Marx directly criticizes the socialism of Fourier, Proudhon, and others who held similar opinions.

"The radical evil of our industrial system is the employment of the laborer in a single occupation, which runs the risk of coming to a stand-still."

Socialism Is the Community of All Classes

Charles Fourier

Like other utopian socialists, Charles Fourier (1772-1837) considered "civilization" repressive and destructive of human happiness. He therefore advocated the formation of communes (Phalansteries) which would be limited in size and characterized by a rigid occupational balance. Because of Fourier's extreme distaste for revolutionary violence, he supported education as a method for achieving his proposed goal. He presented his ideas in several works which include *Treatise on Domestic Agricultural Association* and *The New Industrial World*. In the following viewpoint, Fourier describes the size and makeup of a typical commune (Phalanx) and explains why working conditions on a commune would be more desirable than those under the industrial system.

As you read, consider the following questions:

1. How, according to the author, would people be paid for their work in the typical commune (Phalanx)?
2. What kind of people, in terms of skills and training, does the author believe would live in the commune?

Charles Fourier, *Design For Utopia: Selected Writings of Charles Fourier*, New York: Schocken Books, 1971. Reprinted with permission.

It is necessary for a company of 1,500 to 1,600 persons to have a stretch of land comprising a good square league, say a surface of six million square *toises* (do not let us forget that a third of that would suffice for the simple mode).

The land should be provided with a fine stream of water; it should be intersected by hills, and adapted to varied cultivation; it should be contiguous to a forest, and not far removed from a large city, but sufficiently so to escape intruders....

A Mixed Group

A company will be collected consisting of from 1,500 to 1,600 persons of graduated degrees of fortune, age, character, of theoretical and practical knowledge; care will be taken to secure the greatest amount of variety possible, for the greater the number of variations either in the passions or the faculties of the members, the easier will it be to make them harmonize in a short space of time.

In this district devoted to experiment, there ought to be combined every species of practicable cultivation, including that in conservatories and hot-houses; in addition, there ought to be at least three accessory factories, to be used in winter and on rainy days; furthermore, various practical branches of science and the arts, independent of the schools [universities].

Above all, it will be necessary to fix the valuation of the capital invested in shares; lands, materials, flocks, implements, etc. This point ought, it seems, to be among the first to receive attention; I think it best to dismiss it here. I shall limit myself to remarking that all these investments in transferable shares and stock-coupons will be represented.

A great difficulty to be overcome in the experimental Phalanx will be the formation of the ties of high mechanism or collective bonds of the Series, before the close of the first season. It will be necessary to accomplish the passional union of the mass of the members; to lead them to collective and individual devotion to the maintenance of the Phalanx, and, especially, to perfect harmony regarding the division of the profits, according to the three factors, *Capital, Labor, Talent*. [Income on the Phalanx will be unequal.]...

Capitalists Needed

Let us proceed with the details of composition.

At least seven-eighths of the members ought to be cultivators and manufacturers; the remainder will consist of capitalists, scholars, and artists.

The Phalanx would be badly graded and difficult to balance, if among its capitalists there were several having 100,000 francs, several 50,000 francs, without intermediate fortunes. In such a case it would be necessary to seek to procure intermediate fortunes of 60,000, 70,000, 80,000, 90,000 francs. The Phalanx best graduated in every respect raises social harmony and profits to the highest degree....

Associative labor, in order to exert a strong attraction upon people, will have to differ in every particular from the repulsive conditions which render it so odious in the existing state of things. It is necessary, in order that it become attractive, that associative labor fulfil the following seven conditions:

1. That every laborer be a partner, remunerated by dividends and not by wages.

2. That every one, man, woman, or child, be remunerated in proportion to the three faculties, *capital, labor,* and *talent.*

3. That the industrial sessions be varied about eight times a day, it being impossible to sustain enthusiasm longer than an hour and a half or two hours in the exercise of agricultural or manufacturing labor.

The New Order

In this new order, people possess a guarantee of well-being, of a minimum sufficient for the present and the future, and that this guarantee free them from all uneasiness concerning themselves and their families.

Charles Fourier.

---

4. That they be carried on by bands of friends, united spontaneously, interested and stimulated by very active rivalries.

5. That the workshops and husbandry offer the laborer the allurements of elegance and cleanliness.

6. That the division of labor be carried to the last degree, so that each sex and age may devote itself to duties that are suited to it.

7. That in this distribution, each one, man, woman, or child, be in full enjoyment of the right to labor or the right to engage in such branch of labor as they may please to select, provided they give proof of integrity and ability.

Finally, that, in this new order, people possess a guarantee of well-being, of a minimum sufficient for the present and the future, and that this guarantee free them from all uneasiness concerning themselves and their families....

Enjoyable and Guaranteed Work

The chief source of light-heartedness among Harmonians is the frequent change of sessions. Life is a perpetual torment to our workmen, who are obliged to spend twelve, and frequently fifteen, consecutive hours in some tedious labor. Even ministers are not exempt; we find some of them complain of having passed an entire day in the stupefying task of affixing signatures to thousands of official vouchers. Such wearisome duties are unknown in the associative order; the Harmonians, who devote an hour, an hour and a half, or at most two hours, to the different sessions, and who, in these short sessions, are sustained by cabalistic impulses and by friendly union with selected associates, cannot fail to bring and to find cheerfulness everywhere....

The radical evil of our industrial system is the employment of the laborer in a single occupation, which runs the risk of coming to a stand-still. The fifty thousand workmen of Lyons who are beggars to-day (besides fifty thousand women and children), would be scattered over two or three hundred phalanxes, which would make silk their principal article of manufacture, and which would not be thrown out by a year or two of stagnation in that branch of industry. If at the end of that time their factory should fail completely, they would start one of a different kind, without having stopped work, without ever making their daily subsistence dependent upon a continuation or suspension of outside orders.

"[Man] wishes to labor when he pleases, where he pleases, and as much as he pleases."

Socialism Is the Community of One

Pierre Joseph Proudhon

A leading French radical, Pierre Joseph Proudhon (1809-1865) was the author of numerous influential works on socialism. Unlike most utopian socialists who advocated the formation of cooperative communes, he favored a society composed totally of small holdings, each individually owned and operated. In the following viewpoint taken from his most famous work, *What Is Property?*, Proudhon attacks what he calls "property and communism." By "property," he is referring to a type of agrarian capitalism in which an absentee landlord derives "unearned" profits from the labors of tenant farmers and renters. By communism, he means a societal arrangement where people work according to their abilities and receive according to their needs. "Liberty," Proudhon's ideal society, would combine the best elements of the above two.

As you read, consider the following questions:

1. What are the strengths and weaknesses of communism, according to the author?
2. Why does the author believe that property is an exploitation of the weak?
3. What does Proudhon mean by equality?

Pierre Joseph Proudhon, *What Is Property? An Inquiry into the Principle of Right and Government*, New York: Humboldt Pub. Co., 1892.

I ought not to conceal the fact that property and communism have been considered always the only possible forms of society. This deplorable error has been the life of property. The disadvantages of communism are so obvious that its critics never have needed to employ much eloquence to thoroughly disgust men with it....

Communism is inequality, but not as property is. Property is the exploitation of the weak by the strong. Communism is the exploitation of the strong by the weak. In property, inequality of conditions is the result of force, under whatever name it be disguised: physical and mental force; force of events, chance, *fortune*; force of accumulated property, etc. In communism, inequality springs from placing mediocrity on a level with excellence....

Undesirability of Communism

Communism is oppression and slavery. Man is very willing to obey the law of duty, serve his country, and oblige his friends; but he wishes to labor when he pleases, where he pleases, and as much as he pleases. He wishes to dispose of his own time, to be governed only by necessity, to choose his friendships, his recreation, and his discipline; to act from judgment, not by command; to sacrifice himself through selfishness, not through servile obligation. Communism is essentially opposed to the free exercise of our faculties, to our noblest desires, to our deepest feelings. Any plan which could be devised for reconciling it with the demands of the individual reason and will would end only in changing the thing while preserving the name. Now, if we are honest truth-seekers, we shall avoid disputes about words.

Thus, communism violates the sovereignty of the conscience and equality: the first, by restricting spontaneity of mind and heart, and freedom of thought and action; the second, by placing labor and laziness, skill and stupidity, and even vice and virtue on an equality in point of comfort.* For the rest, if property is impossible on account of the desire to accumulate, communism would soon become so through the desire to shirk....

Liberty: The Alternative

Communism seeks *equality* and *law*. Property, born of the sovereignty of the reason, and the sense of personal merit, wishes above all things *independence* and *proportionality*.

But communism, mistaking uniformity for law, and levelism for equality, becomes tyrannical and unjust. Property, by its despotism and encroachments, soon proves itself oppressive and anti-social.

The objects of communism and property are good—their results are bad. And why? Because both are exclusive, and each disregards

*Proudhon is referring here to the communist adage: "From each according to ability, to each according to need."

25

two elements of society. Communism rejects independence and proportionality; property does not satisfy equality and law.

Now, if we imagine a society based upon these four principles,—equality, law, independence, and proportionality,—we find:—

1. That *equality*, consisting only in *equality of conditions*, that is, *of means*, and not in *equality of comfort*,—which it is the business of the laborers to achieve for themselves, when provided with equal means,—in no way violates justice and *équité*.

2. That *law*, resulting from the knowledge of facts, and consequently based upon necessity itself, never clashes with independence.

3. That individual *independence*, or the autonomy of the private reason, originating in the difference in talents and capacities, can exist without danger within the limits of the law.

Property and Exploitation

Centralize property in the hands of a few and the millions are under bondage to property—a bondage as absolute and deplorable as if their limbs were covered with manacles.

Lewis Henry Morgan, "Diffusion Against Centralization," 1852.

---

4. That *proportionality*, being admitted only in the sphere of intelligence and sentiment, and not as regards material objects, may be observed without violating justice or social equality.

This third form of society, the synthesis of communism and property, we will call *liberty*.

In determining the nature of liberty, we do not unite communism and property indiscriminately; such a process would be absurd....We search by analysis for those elements in each which are true, and in harmony with the laws of Nature and society, disregarding the rest altogether; and the result gives us an adequate expression of the natural form of human society,—in one word, liberty.

"It is only our species that has introduced this murderous folly of making distinctions in merit and value."

Socialism Is the Community of Equals

"Gracchus" Babeuf

Francois Noel Babeuf (1760-1797), more commonly known as "Gracchus" Babeuf, was a late eighteenth-century French radical. Originally an enthusiastic supporter of the French Revolution, he later became a bitter enemy of the revolutionary government. Claiming that the revolution failed to establish economic equality, Babeuf eventually formed a secret society that plotted to overthrow the government. (The plot became known as the Conspiracy of the Equals.) The plot was betrayed from within and Babeuf was brought to trial, found guilty of conspiracy, and executed. In the following viewpoint, he attempts to justify his belief in the absolute equality of all peoples.

As you read, consider the following questions:

1. Why does the author believe that more capable individuals should not receive additional compensation for their work efforts?
2. According to the author, what should be one of the most important elements of a society's social institutions?
3. Do you find the author's arguments logical? Why or why not?

Excerpts From SOCIALIST THOUGHT, A DOCUMENTARY HISTORY edited by Albert Fried and Ronald Sanders. Copyright © 1964 by Albert Fried and Ronald Sanders. Reprinted by permission of Doubleday & Company, Inc.

The superiority of talents and of efforts is only a chimera and a specious trap, which has always unduly served the schemes of the conspirators against the equality and welfare of men.

It is both absurd and unjust to pretend that a greater recompense is due someone whose task demands a higher degree of intelligence, a greater amount of application and mental strain; none of this in any way expands the capacity of his stomach.

Necessity of Sharing

No grounds whatever can justify pretension to a recompense beyond what is sufficient for individaul needs.

Such a pretension is nothing but a matter of opinion, in no way validated by reason, and perhaps—it remains to be seen—not even valid in accordance with a principle of force, at least of a force purely natural and physical in nature.

It is only those who are intelligent who have fixed such a high price upon the conceptions of their brains, and if the physically strong had been able to keep up with them in regulating the order of things, they would no doubt have established the merit of the arm to be as great as that of the head, and the fatigue of the entire body would have been offered as sufficient compensation for the fatigue of the small part of it that ruminates.

If this principle of equalization is not posited, then the most intelligent and the most industrious are given a warrant for hoarding, a title to despoil with impunity all those who are less gifted.

Thus the equilibrium of well-being in the social state is destroyed, is overthrown, since nothing has been better proven than this maxim: *that one succeeds in having too much only by causing others not to have enough.*

All our civil institutions, our reciprocal transactions, are nothing but acts of perpetual brigandage, authorized by barbarous laws, under whose sway we are occupied only in tearing each other apart.

Our society of swindlers brings all sorts of vice, crime and misfortune in the wake of its atrocious primordial conventions, against which good men ally themselves in a vain attempt to make war upon them. In this they cannot be victorious because they do not attack the evil at its roots, because their measures are only palliatives drawn from the reservoir of false ideas created by our organic depravity.

True Justice

It is clear, then, from all that has been said, that everything owned by those who have more than their individual due of society's goods, is theft and usurpation.

It is therefore just to take it back from them.

Even someone who could prove that he is capable, by the individual exertion of his own natural strength, of doing the work of four men, and so lay claim to the recompense of four, would be no less a conspirator against society, because he would be upsetting the equilibrium of things by this alone, and would thus be destroying the precious principle of equality.

Wisdom imperiously demands of all the members of the association that they suppress such a man, that they pursue him as a scourge of society, that they at least reduce him to a state whereby he can do the work of only one man, so that he will be able to demand the recompense of only one man.

It is only our species that has introduced this murderous folly of making distinctions in merit and value, and it is our species alone that knows misfortune and privation.

There must exist no form of privation but the one that nature imposes upon everyone as a result of some unavoidable accident, in which case these privations must be borne by everyone and divided up equally among them.

The products of industry and of genius also become the property of all, the domain of the entire association, from the very moment that the workers and the inventors have created them, because they are simply compensation for earlier discoveries made through genius and industry, from which the new inventors and workers have profited within the framework of social life, and which have helped them to make their discoveries.

Fruits for All

The first man who, after enclosing a plot of land, saw fit to say: "This is mine," and found people who were simple enough to believe him, was the true founder of civil society. How many crimes, wars, murders, sufferings and horrors mankind would have been spared if someone had torn up the stakes or filled up the moat and cried to his fellows: "Don't listen to this impostor; you are lost if you forget that the earth belongs to no one, and that its fruits are for all!"

Jean Jacques Rousseau, *Discourse on the Origin of Inequality Among Men,* 1755.

Since the knowledge acquired is the domain of everyone, it must therefore be equally distributed among everyone.

A truth that has been impertinently contested by bad faith, by prejudice, by thoughtlessness, is the fact that this equal distribution of knowledge among everyone would make all men nearly equal in capacity and even in talent.

Education is a monstrosity when it is unequal, when it is the exclusive patrimony of a portion of the association: because then it becomes, in the hands of this portion, an accumulation of machinery, an arsenal of all sorts of weapons that helps this portion of society to make war against the other, which is unarmed, and to succeed thereby in strangling it, deceiving it, stripping it bare, and shackling it down to the most shameful servitude.

There are no truths more important than those that one philosopher has proclaimed in these terms: "Declaim as much as you wish on the subject of the best form of government, you will still have nothing at all so long as you have not destroyed the seeds of cupidity and ambition."

Essentials of Equality

It is therefore necessary that the social institutions be such that they eradicate within every last individual the hope that he might ever become richer, more powerful, or more distinguished because of his talents, than any of his equals.

To be more specific, it is necessary to *bind together everyone's lot;* to render the lot of each member of the association independent of chance, and of happy or unfavorable circumstance; *to assure to every man and to his posterity, no matter how numerous it may be, as much as they need, but no more than they need;* and to shut off from everybody all the possible paths by which they might obtain some part of the products of nature and of work that is more than their individual due.

The sole means of arriving at this is to establish a *common administration;* to suppress private property; to place every man of talent in the line of work he knows best; to oblige him to deposit the fruit of his work in the common store, to establish a simple *administration of needs*, which, keeping a record of all individuals and all the things that are available to them, will distribute these available goods with the most scrupulous equality, and will see to it that they make their way into the home of every citizen.

30

"The new Christian organization will....direct all its institutions...towards the advancement of the well-being of the poorest class."

Socialism Is the Community of Christians

Claude Henri Saint-Simon

Claude Henri Saint-Simon (1760-1825) was a French social philosopher. He believed that a utopian society was possible if the intelligentsia of his day, the scientists and industrialists, would apply a series of "scientific" principles he formulated to the reorganization of society. In his book, *The New Christianity*, he argued that the concept of universal brotherhood *must* accompany this scientific reorganization. Among other things, his ideas called for public control of the means of production and the emancipation of women. The following viewpoint, excerpted from *The New Christianity*, was written in dialogue form. In it, the conversers, a "conservative" and an "innovator," discuss the role of Christianity in the new social order.

As you read, consider the following questions:

1. According to the author, what principle will govern the temporal and spiritual institutions of the new Christianity?
2. Why does the author address his remarks to industrialists, scholars and artists?
3. What does the author believe the role of "princes" and world leaders should be in his Christian society?

Excerpts from SOCIALIST THOUGHT, A DOCUMENTARY HISTORY edited by Albert Fried and Ronald Sanders. Copyright © 1964 by Albert Fried and Ronald Sanders. Reprinted by permission of Doubleday & Company, Inc.

The Conservative: Do you believe in God?

The Innovator: Yes, I believe in God.

The C.: Do you believe that the Christian religion has a divine origin?

The I.: Yes, I believe that....

Fundamental Principles

C.: Do you recognize the Church as a divine institution?

I.: I believe that God Himself founded the Christian Church; I am filled with the deepest respect and the greatest admiration for the conduct of the Fathers of this Church.

These leaders of the primitive Church explicitly preached the unity of all peoples. They tried to get them to live at peace with one another; they proclaimed positively and most energetically to the rich and powerful that it was their first duty to employ all their resources in bringing about the promptest possible amelioration of the physical and moral existence of the poor.

These leaders of the primitive Church produced the best book that has ever been published, the *Primitive Catechism*, in which they divided the activities of men into two classes, the good and the bad—that is, into those activities that conform to the fundamental principle of divine morality, and those contrary to this principle....

C.: What will become of the Christian religion if...the men charged with the task of teaching it have become heretics?

I.: Christianity will become the sole, universal religion; the Asians and Africans will convert to it; the members of the European clergy will become good Christians, and will abandon the various heresies that they profess today. The true doctrine of Christianity, that is, the most general doctrine that can be derived from the fundamental principle of divine morality, will be produced, and the differences in religious opinions that exist right now will immediately come to an end.

The first Christian doctrine to appear in history gave society only a partial and quite incomplete organization. The rights of Caesar remained independent of the rights assigned to the Church. *Render unto Caesar the things that are Caesar's;* so goes the famous maxim that separated these two powers. The temporal power continued to base itself upon the law of the strongest, while the Church maintained that society should recognize as legitimate only those institutions that had the amelioration of the existence of the poorest class as their object.

The new Christian organization will derive its temporal as well as its spiritual institutions from the principle that *all men must behave as brothers toward one another*. It will direct all its institutions, whatever their nature, towards the advancement of the well-being of the poorest class.

C.: On what facts do you base this opinion? By what authority are you able to believe that a single moral principle will become

32

the sole regulator of all human societies?

I.: The most general principle, the principle of divine morality, is the one that must become the sole moral principle; this is the consequence of its nature and origin.

The people of God, that people who received divine revelation before the appearance of Jesus, and who are the most widely spread out over the surface of the earth, have always felt that the Christian doctrine, founded by the Fathers of the Church, was incomplete. They have always maintained that a great era is yet to come, an era to which they have given the name *messianic*, in which the religious doctrine would be presented in all the universality of which it is capable; that it would govern equally the activities of the temporal and the spiritual powers, and that all the races of man would henceforth have only one single religion, one common organization....

Gospel of Greed

The gospel of Christ says that progress comes from every individual merging his individuality in sympathy with his neighbors. On the other side, the conviction of the nineteenth century is that progress takes place by virtue of every individual's striving for himself with all his might and trampling his neighbor under foot whenever he gets a chance to do so. This may accurately be called the Gospel of Greed.

Charles S. Pierce, "Evolutionary Love," *The Monist*, III, June 1893.

C.: I have several observations to make on the general nature of your efforts. The new formula under which you represent the principle of Christianity includes your entire system of social organization, a system founded at once upon philosophical considerations from the sciences, the fine arts, industry, and the religious sentiment that is the most widespread in the civilized world, that of Christianity. Why, then, have you not presented this system, this object of all your reflections, first and foremost from the religious point of view, from the point of view that is at once the most elevated and the most popular? Why have you addressed yourself to industrialists, scholars and artists, instead of going directly to the people with a religious message?...

I.: I had to address myself first to the rich and powerful, to see to it that they became favorably disposed toward the new doctrine, by making them realize that it was in no way contrary to their interests, since it clearly would be impossible to ameliorate the moral and physical existence of the poor classes by any other means than those that tend to advance the well-being of the rich classes.

I had to make artists, men of learning and the chiefs of industrial enterprises realize that their interests were essentially the same as those of the great masses of people; that they themselves belonged to the class of laborers at the same time that they were its natural leaders; that the approbation of the masses for the services these men rendered them was the sole recompense worthy of their glorious efforts. I had to insist strongly upon this point, since it is of the greatest importance, and is the sole means of providing the nations with the sort of guides that truly deserve their confidence, guides capable of leading public opinion and enabling it to judge sanely what political measures are either favorable or contrary to the interests of the greatest number. Finally, I had to make Catholics and Protestants see exactly when it was that they had started down a false path, so as to facilitate the means of bringing them back onto the true one. I must insist upon this point, because the conversion of the Catholic and Protestant clergies would provide the New Christianity with great sources of strength....

A Divine Mission

Yes, I believe Christianity to be a divine institution, and I am persuaded that God grants special protection to those who devote their efforts to causing all human institutions to be submitted to the fundamental principle of this sublime doctrine. I am convinced that I myself am performing a divine mission when I remind the Peoples and the Kings of the true spirit of Christianity. And, fully confident of the special and divine protection that is being given to my efforts, I therefore feel hardy enough to make representations concerning their conduct to the Kings of Europe, who have formed a coalition, and have given this union the sacred name of *Holy Alliance;* I now address myself directly to them, and dare to say:

PRINCES,

What is the nature, what is the character, in the eyes of God and of Christians, of the power that you exercise?

What are the bases of the system of social organization that you are working to establish? What measures have you taken to ameliorate the moral and physical existence of the poor classes?

You call yourselves Christians, yet you continue to base your power upon physical force, so that you are still only the successors of Caesar, and you forget that true Christians propose, as the final outcome of their efforts, to annihilate completely the power of the sword, the power of Caesar, which, by its very nature, is provisional....

Listen to the voice of God, which speaks to you through my lips; become good Christians once again, and stop looking upon armies, noblemen, heretical clergies and perverse judges as your principal sources of sustenance. United under the banner of Christianity, you will be able to accomplish all the duties that this banner imposes upon the powerful.

"The New System is founded on principles which will enable mankind to prevent...*the evils and miseries which...our forefathers have experienced."*

Socialism Is the Community of a New World Order

Robert Owen

Robert Owen (1771-1858) was a British social reformer and socialist. The son of a saddler, he began working in the textile industry at the age of ten and eventually became a successful and prominent cotton manufacturer in Manchester, England. However, unlike most manufacturers of his day, he channeled the profits of his business toward the betterment of the working and living conditions of his workers. In 1800, he purchased a factory in New Lanark, Scotland and successfully converted New Lanark into a model industrial town. Owen based his philanthropy upon the belief that environment molds individual character and that environment can be appreciably improved by the cooperative efforts of all classes of society. The following viewpoint outlines his philosophy.

As you read, consider the following questions:

1. What are the three "first principles" upon which Owen claims all existing and past societies are based?
2. Why does the author believe that societal reform should be gradual in nature?

Robert Owen in a speech presented before the town of New Lanark, Scotland in 1816 on the occasion of the opening of the "Institution for the Formation of Character."

Every society which exists at present, as well as every society which history records, has been formed and governed on a belief in the following notions, assumed as *first principles:*

First,—That it is in the power of every individual to form his own character.

Hence the various systems called by the name of religion, codes of law, and punishments. Hence also the angry passions entertained by individuals and nations towards each other.

Second,—That the affections are at the command of the individual.

Hence insincerity and degradation of character. Hence the miseries of domestic life, and more than one-half of all the crimes of mankind.

Third,—That it is necessary that a large portion of mankind should exist in ignorance and poverty, in order to secure to the remaining part such a degree of happiness as they now enjoy.

Hence a system of counteraction in the pursuits of men, a general opposition among individuals to the interests of each other, and the necessary effects of such a system,—ignorance, poverty, and vice.

The True Facts

Facts prove, however—

First,—That character is universally formed *for*, and not *by*, the individual.

Second,—That *any* habits and sentiments may be given to mankind.

Third,—That the affections are *not* under the control of the individual.

Fourth,—That every individual may be trained to produce far more than he can consume, while there is a sufficiency of soil left for him to cultivate.

Fifth,—That nature has provided means by which population may be at all times maintained in the proper state to give the greatest happiness to every individual, without one check of vice or misery.

Sixth,—That any community may be arranged, on a due combination of the foregoing principles, in such a manner, as not only to withdraw vice, poverty, and, in a great degree, misery, from the world, but also to place *every* individual under circumstances in which he shall enjoy more permanent happiness than can be given to *any* individual under the principles which have hitherto regulated society.

Seventh,—That all the assumed fundamental principles on which society has hitherto been founded are erroneous, and may be demonstrated to be contrary to fact. And—

Eighth,—That the change which would follow the abandonment of those erroneous maxims which bring misery into the world, and the adoption of principles of truth, unfolding a system which shall

36

remove and for ever exclude that misery, may be effected without the slightest injury to any human being.

Here is the groundwork,—these are the data, on which society shall ere long be re-arranged; and for this simple reason, that it will be rendered evident that it will be for the immediate and future interest of every one to lend his most active assistance gradually to reform society on this basis. I say *gradually*, for in that word the most important considerations are involved. Any sudden and coercive attempt which may be made to remove even misery from men will prove injurious rather than beneficial. Their minds must be gradually prepared by an essential alteration of the circumstances which surround them, for any great and important change and amelioration in their condition. They must be first convinced of their blindness: this cannot be effected, even among the least unreasonable, or those termed the best part of mankind, in their present state, without creating some degree of irritation. This irritation, must then be tranquillized before another step ought to be attempted; and a general conviction must be established of the truth of the principles on which the project change is to be founded. Their introduction into practice will then become easy,—difficulties will vanish as we approach them,—and, afterwards, the desire to see the whole system carried immediately into effect will exceed the means of putting it into execution....

Object of the State

The object of the State is precisely this, to place the individuals *through this* union in a position to attain to *such objects*, and reach such a *stage of existence* as they *never* could have reached as individuals; to make them capable of acquiring an amount of *education, power,* and *freedom* which would have been wholly unattainable by them as individuals.

Ferdinand Lassalle, *The Working Class Program*, 1862.

Under this system, before commands are issued it shall be known whether they can or cannot be obeyed. Men shall not be called upon to assent to doctrines and to dogmas which do not carry conviction to their minds. They shall not be taught that merit can exist in doing, or that demerit can arise from not doing that over which they have no control. They shall not be told, as at present, that they must love that which, by the constitution of their nature, they are compelled to dislike. They shall not be trained in wild imaginary notions, that inevitably make them despise and hate all mankind out of the little narrow circle in which they exist, and then be told that they must heartily and sincerely love all their fellow-men. No, my friends, that system which shall make its way into the heart of every man, is founded upon principles which have not the slightest resemblance to any of those I have alluded to. On the contrary, it is directly opposed to them; and the effects it will produce in practice will differ as much from the practice which history records, and from that which we see around us, as hypocrisy, hatred, envy, revenge, wars, poverty, injustice, oppression, and all their consequent misery, differ from that genuine charity and sincere kindness of which we perpetually hear, but which we have never seen, and which, under the existing systems, we never can see.

Charity and Kindness

That charity and that kindness admit of no exception. They extend to every child of man, however he may have been taught, however he may have been trained. They consider not what country gave him birth, what may be his complexion, what his habits or his sentiments. Genuine charity and true kindness instruct, that whatever these may be, should they prove the very reverse of what we have been taught to think right and best, our conduct towards him, our sentiments with respect to him, should undergo no change; for, when we shall see things as they really are, we shall know that this our fellow-man has undergone the same kind of process and training from infancy which we have experienced; that he has been as effectually taught to deem his sentiments and actions right, as we have been to imagine ours right and his wrong; when perhaps the only difference is, that we were born in one country, and he in another. If this be not true, then indeed are all our prospects hopeless; then fierce contentions, poverty, and vice, must continue for ever. Fortunately, however, there is now a superabundance of facts to remove all doubt from every mind; and the principles may now be fully developed, which will easily explain the source of all the opinions which now perplex and divide the world; and their source being discovered, mankind may withdraw all those which are false and injurious, and prevent any evil from arising in consequence of the varieties of sentiments, or rather of feelings, which may afterwards remain.

The New Order

In short, my friends, the New System is founded on principles which will enable mankind to *prevent*, in the rising generation, almost all, if not all of the evils and miseries which we and our forefathers have experienced. A correct knowledge of human nature will be acquired; ignorance will be removed; the angry passions will be prevented from gaining any strength; charity and kindness will universally prevail; poverty will not be known; the interest of each individual will be in strict unison with the interest of every individual in the world. There will not be any counteraction of wishes and desires among men. Temperance and simplicity of manners will be the characteristics of every part of society. The natural defects of the few will be amply compensated by the increased attention and kindness towards them of the many. None will have cause to complain; for each will possess, without injury to another, all that can tend to his comfort, his well-being, and his happiness.—Such will be the certain consequences of the introduction into practice of that system for which I have been silently preparing the way for upwards of five-and-twenty years.

"The bourgeoisie naturally conceives the world in which it is supreme to be the best."

Socialism Is the Community of Workers

Karl Marx

Karl Marx (1818-1883) is considered the father of modern scientific socialism. A native of Prussia, Marx was convinced that all major historical change resulted from class conflict. He therefore preached that a socialistic society could be realized only through the revolutionary activity of the workers of the world. The following viewpoint, excerpted from *The Manifesto of the Communist Party*, was written by Marx on the basis of a draft prepared by his friend and sometimes collaborator, Friedrich Engels. In it, Marx criticizes two of the earlier schools of socialist thought which he labels "petty-bourgeois socialism" and "utopian socialism." He believed that the first was reactionary in that it aspired to restore "the old means of production and of exchange." The second he considered unacceptable because the present ruling class would be included in its revamping of society.

As you read, consider the following questions:

1. What criticisms does Marx have of "petty-bourgeois socialism"?
2. How does he describe "utopian socialism"?

Karl Marx and Friedrich Engels, *The Manifesto of the Communist Party*, Peking: Foreign Language Press, 1970.

In countries like France, where the peasants constitute far more than half of the population, it was natural that writers who sided with the proletariat against the bourgeoisie, should use, in their criticism of the bourgeois *regime*, the standard of the peasant and petty bourgeois, and from the standpoint of these intermediate classes should take up the cudgels for the working class. Thus arose petty-bourgeois Socialism....

This school of Socialism dissected with great acuteness the contradictions in the conditions of modern production. It laid bare the hypocritical apologies of economists. It proved, incontrovertibly, the disastrous effects of machinery and division of labour; the concentration of capital and land in a few hands; overproduction and crises; it pointed out the inevitable ruin of the petty bourgeois and peasant, the misery of the proletariat, the anarchy in production, the crying inequalities in the distribution of wealth, the industrial war of extermination between nations, the dissolution of old moral bonds, of the old family relations, of the old nationalities.

In its positive aims, however, this form of Socialism aspires either to restoring the old means of production and of exchange, and with them the old property relations, and the old society, or to cramping the modern means of production and of exchange, within the framework of the old property relations that have been, and were bound to be, exploded by those means. In either case, it is both reactionary and Utopian.

Its last words are: corporate guilds for manufacture; patriarchal relations in agriculture.

Ultimately, when stubborn historical facts had dispersed all intoxicating effects of self-deception, this form of Socialism ended in a miserable fit of the blues....

Proudhon and Others

This form of Socialism has, moreover, been worked out into complete systems.

We may cite Proudhon...as an example of this form.

The Socialistic bourgeois want all the advantages of modern social conditions without the struggles and dangers necessarily resulting therefrom. They desire the existing state of society minus its revolutionary and disintegrating elements. They wish for a bourgeoisie without a proletariat. The bourgeoisie naturally conceives the world in which it is supreme to be the best; and bourgeois Socialism develops this comfortable conception into various more or less complete systems. In requiring the proletariat to carry out such a system, and thereby to march straightway into the social New Jerusalem, it but requires in reality, that the proletariat should remain within the bounds of existing society, but should cast away all its hateful ideas concerning the bourgeoisie....

The Socialist and Communist systems properly so called, those of St. Simon, Fourier, Owen and others, spring into existence in the

41

Karl Marx

early undeveloped period...of the struggle between proletariat and bourgeoisie....

The founders of these systems see, indeed, the class antagonisms, as well as the action of the decomposing elements in the prevailing form of society. But the proletariat, as yet in its infancy, offers to them the spectacle of a class without any historical initiative or any independent political movement.

Since the development of class antagonism keeps even pace with the development of industry, the economic situation, as they find it, does not as yet offer to them the material conditions for the emancipation of the proletariat. They therefore search after a new social science, after new social laws, that are to create these conditions....

In the formation of their plans they are conscious of caring chiefly for the interests of the working class, as being the most suffering class. Only from the point of view of being the most suffering class does the proletariat exist for them.

The undeveloped state of the class struggle, as well as their own surroundings, causes Socialists of this kind to consider themselves far superior to all class antagonisms. They want to improve the condition of every member of society, even that of the most favoured. Hence, they habitually appeal to society at large, without distinction of class; nay, by preference, to the ruling class. For how can people, when once they understand their system, fail to see in it the best possible plan of the best possible state of society?

Hence, they reject all political, and especially all revolutionary, action; they wish to attain their ends by peaceful means, and endeavour, by small experiments, necessarily doomed to failure, and by the force of example, to pave the way for the new social Gospel.

Such fantastic pictures of future society, painted at a time when the proletariat is still in a very undeveloped state and has but a fantastic conception of its own position, correspond with the first instinctive yearnings of that class for a general reconstruction of society.

Out of Touch with Reality

But these Socialist and Communist publications contain also a critical element. They attack every principle of existing society. Hence they are full of the most valuable materials for the enlightenment of the working class. The practical measures proposed in them—such as the abolition of the distinction between town and country, of the family, of the carrying on of industries for the account of private individuals, and of the wage system, the proclamation of social harmony, the conversion of the functions of the State into a mere superintendence of production, all these proposals point solely to the disappearance of class antagonisms which were, at that time, only just cropping up, and which, in these publications, are recognised in their earliest, indistinct and undefined forms only. These proposals, therefore, are of a purely Utopian character.

The significance of Critical-Utopian Socialism and Communism bears an inverse relation to historical development. In proportion as the modern class struggle develops and takes definite shape, this fantastic standing apart from the contest, these fantastic attacks on it, lose all practical value and all theoretical justification. Therefore, although the originators of these systems were, in many respects, revolutionary, their disciples have, in every case, formed mere reactionary sects. They hold fast by the original views of their masters, in opposition to the progressive historical development of the proletariat. They, therefore, endeavour, and that consistently, to deaden the class struggle and to reconcile the class antagonisms. They still dream of experimental realisation of their social Utopias, of founding isolated *"phalansteres,"* of establishing "Home Colonies," of setting up a "Little Icaria"...and to realise all these castles in the air, they are compelled to appeal to the feelings and purses of the bourgeois. By degrees they sink into the category of the reactionary conservative Socialists depicted above, differing from these only by more systematic pedantry, and by their fanatical and superstitious belief in the miraculous effects of their social science.

They, therefore, violently oppose all political action on the part of the working class; such action, according to them, can only result from blind unbelief in the new Gospel.

Distinguishing Between Fact and Opinion

This activity is designed to help develop the basic reading and thinking skill of distinguishing between fact and opinion. Consider the following statement as an example: "Utopian socialists think about and develop ideas for a new society." This statement is a factual one describing something utopian socialists do. But the statement "utopian socialists have unrealistic and dangerous ideas" is clearly an opinion of utopian ideas.

When investigating controversial issues it is important that one be able to distinguish between statements of fact and statements of opinion. It is also important to recognize that not all statements of fact are true. They may appear to be true, but some are based on inaccurate or false information. For this activity, however, we are concerned with understanding the difference between those statements which appear to be factual and those which appear to be based primarily on opinion.

Most of the following statements are taken from the viewpoints in this chapter. Consider each statement carefully. *Mark O for any statement you believe is an opinion or interpretation of facts. Mark F for any statement you believe is a fact.*

If you are doing this activity as a member of a class or group, compare your answers with those of other class or group members. Be able to defend your answers. You may discover that others will come to different conclusions than you. Listening to the reasons others present for their answers may give you valuable insights in distinguishing between fact and opinion.

If you are reading this book alone, ask others if they agree with your answers. You too will find this interaction very valuable.

O = opinion
F = fact

1. *Primitive Catechism* is the best book ever published.

2. The New System will enable humankind to prevent almost all of the evils and misery we have experienced.

3. In France the peasants constituted far more than half of the population.

4. Property is the exploitation of the weak by the strong.

5. Utopian communities were founded by people dissatisfied with the lifestyles typical in their society.

6. One succeeds in having too much only by causing others not to have enough.

7. It is in the power of individuals to form their own characters.

8. Communism is essentially opposed to the free exercise of our facilities, to our deepest feelings and desires.

9. Fifty-thousand workmen of Lyons are beggars, besides fifty-thousand women and children.

10. When education is unequal it becomes an arsenal of weapons which helps the educated portion of society to make war against the uneducated, who are unarmed.

11. In the 1870s, life was a perpetual torment to workers, who were obliged to spend twelve, and frequently fifteen, consecutive hours in some tedious labor.

12. Many poor women and children worked for low wages in coal mines in the nineteenth century.

13. The life of a poor person is more difficult than that of a wealthy person.

14. Thousands of families in Africa barely have enough food to survive.

15. Those who are intelligent have fixed a high price on their brains: if the physically strong had been able to regulate things, they would no doubt have established the merit of the arms to be as great as that of the head.

16. Leaders of the primitive Church preached the unity of all peoples and tried to get them to live in peace with one another.

17. True Christians propose to annihilate the power of the sword, the power of Caesar.

18. Today's socialists do not agree entirely with what the utopian socialists wrote over one hundred years ago.

Bibliography

The following bibliography deals with the subject matter of this chapter.

J. Beecher and
R. Bienvenu
The Utopian Vision of Charles Fourier: Selected Texts on Work, Love, and Passionate Attraction. Boston: Beacon Press, 1971.

Paul E. Corcoran
Before Marx: Socialism and Communism in France, 1830-48. New York: St. Martin's Press, 1983.

Edouard Dolleans
Proudhon. Paris: Gallimard, 1968.

Friedrich Engels
Socialism: Utopian and Scientific. New York: International Publishers Co., 1935.

James Joll
The Anarchists. Cambridge, MA: Harvard University Press, 1980.

David McLellan
Marx: The First Hundred Years. New York: St. Martin's Press, 1983.

Stanley Moore
Marx on the Choice Between Socialism and Communism. Cambridge, MA: Harvard University Press, 1980.

Bernard Murchland
The Dream of Christian Socialism. Washington, DC: American Enterprise Institute, 1982.

Robert Owen
A New View of Society and Report to the County of Lanark. Harmondsworth, England: Penguin Books, 1970.

Pierre J. Proudhon
General Idea of the Revolution in the Nineteenth Century. London: Freedom Press, 1923.

Dorothee Soelle
Beyond Mere Dialogue: On Being Christian and Socialist. Pamphlet available from Christians for Socialism, 3540 Fourteenth St., Detroit, MI 48208.

Keith Taylor
The Political Ideas of the Utopian Socialists. Totowa, NJ: Biblio Distribution Centre, 1982.

Paul Thomas
Karl Marx and the Anarchists. Boston: Routledge & Kegan, 1985.

Alan Wolfe
"In Defense of Utopianism," *Dissent*, Summer 1985.

Revisionist Socialism

Introduction

When Karl Marx and Friedrich Engels wrote *The Manifesto of the Communist Party* in 1848, they felt certain that the capitalistic system would soon be replaced by universal socialism. Believing that class conflict was a necessary prerequisite for historical change, they advocated revolutionary activity by the working class as the means to achieve that change. However, in the decades following the publication of the "Manifesto," capitalism did not falter and die out. Instead, it underwent a period of vast expansion. Moreover, the growth of capitalism was accompanied by a gradual improvement in the political and economic conditions of the working class.

Much of this seemed to disprove many of Marx's basic assumptions regarding capitalism and somewhat underminded his credibility in socialist circles. This is not to say that Marx lost complete favor within the socialist movement. Quite the contrary. The general tendencies of economic and social historical development he formulated have remained the movement's guiding credo. What it simply meant was that as a political philosopher, Marx was a poor prophet.

Marx had predicated his belief in the inevitability of revolution upon two key factors, the continued exploitation of the workers and the growing disparity of wealth between the classes. Yet neither of these expectations fully materialized, at least not to the degree predicted by Marx. In countries such as England and the United States, legislation aimed at improving the working and living standards of laborers was being passed with growing frequency. More importantly, millions of workers were gaining the vote, ultimately placing them in a position to elect officials sympathetic to their cause. And accompanying these changes was a phenomenon of perhaps even greater significance, the gradual rise of the middle class. Rather than disappear or remain a negligible force (as Marx believed), the middle class grew in size, affluence, and political consciousness, eventually becoming a buffer between upper and lower classes.

It was because of these changing circumstances that a new school of socialist thought emerged. Referred to as "revisionist socialism" (because it represented a "revision" of key elements in Marxian socialism), the new school was led by Eduard Bernstein in Germany and a society called the Fabian Socialists in England. Bernstein and the Fabians based their revision of Marx upon the latter's erroneous predictions of trends in capitalism. As the conditions of the working class became less acute and, in some cases, even tolerable, and as more and more workers obtained the right to vote, Bernstein and other revisionists began advocating a shift away from revolutionary socialism. They were certain that their ideas were clearly in touch with the times. The stuffing of ballot boxes seemed much more logical than the shedding of blood. Their ultimate goal, the establishment of a socialistic society, remained unchanged. They were simply proposing that the means toward that end be revised to favor nonviolent or evolutionary tactics. By parliamentary democracy, socialism could be realized.

Despite the rationalization of Bernstein, the Fabians, and others, the Marxian socialists were not convinced that socialism could be achieved by peaceful means. Accordingly, they attacked revisionism with the same passion with which Marx had attacked the socialists who preceded him. The following viewpoints are examples of the arguments both for and against evolutionary socialism. They are taken from the works of six of the most influential writers in the history of socialist thought.

"I lay the greatest value...on the political activity of working men in town and country for the interests of their class."

The Reason for Evolutionary Socialism

Eduard Bernstein

Eduard Bernstein (1850-1932) was a leading German socialist and writer. He joined the German Social Democratic party in 1870 and rose to the position of editor of the party's newspaper. Pressured into leaving Germany in the 1880s during a period of antisocialist legislation, he eventually settled in England where he was influenced considerably by that country's parliamentary institutions. In time, Bernstein became convinced that socialism could be achieved in countries like England through legislative rather than revolutionary means. He persuasively set forth his principles in his classic revisionist work, *Evolutionary Socialism*. While his ideas were supported by many socialist groups, they provoked vigorous attacks from traditional Marxist quarters. In the following viewpoint excerpted from *Evolutionary Socialism*, Bernstein points out some basic errors of Karl Marx and provides a rationale for his revisionist philosophy.

As you read, consider the following questions:

1. What criticisms does the author make of *The Communist Manifesto*?
2. How can social democracy be achieved, according to the author?

Eduard Bernstein, *Evolutionary Socialism: A Criticism and Affirmation*, New York: Schocken Books, Inc., 1965. Reprinted with permission.

I set myself against the notion that we have to expect shortly a collapse of the bourgeois economy and that social democracy should be induced by the prospect of such an imminent, great, social catastrophe to adapt its tactics to that assumption. That I maintain most emphatically.

The adherents of this theory of a catastrophe base it especially on the conclusions of *The Communist Manifesto*. This is a mistake in every respect.

The theory which *The Communist Manifesto* sets forth of the evolution of modern society was correct as far as it characterized the general tendencies of that evolution. But it was mistaken in several special deductions, above all in the estimate of the *time* the evolution would take....It is evident that if social evolution takes a much greater period of time than was assumed, it must also take upon itself *forms* and lead to forms that were not foreseen and could not be foreseen then.

Social conditions have not developed to such an acute opposition of things and classes as is depicted in the *Manifesto*. It is not only useless, it is the greatest folly to attempt to conceal this from ourselves. The number of members of the possessing classes is today not smaller but larger. The enormous increase of social wealth is not accompanied by a decreasing number of large capitalists but by an increasing number of capitalists of all degrees. The middle classes change their character, but they do not disappear from the social scale....

Evolutionary Democracy

In all advanced countries, we see the privileges of the capitalist bourgeoisie yielding step by step to democratic organizations. Under the influence of this, and driven by the movement of the working classes which is daily becoming stronger, a social reaction has set in against the exploiting tendencies of capital, a counter-action which, although it still proceeds timidly and feebly, yet does exist and is always drawing more departments of economic life under its influence. Factory legislation, the democratization of local government, and the extension of its area of work, the freeing of trade unions and systems of cooperative trade from legal restrictions, the consideration of standard conditions of labour in the work undertaken by public authorities—all these characterize this phase of the evolution.

But the more the political organizations of the modern nations are democratized the more the needs and opportunities of great political catastrophes are diminished. He who holds firmly to the catastrophic theory of evolution must, with all his power, withstand and hinder the evolution described above, which, indeed, the logical defender of that theory formerly did. But is the conquest of political power by the proletariat simply to be by a political catastrophe? Is it to be the appropriation and utilization of the power of the state by the proletariat exclusively against the whole nonproletarian world?

If not...one cannot reasonably take any offense if it is declared that for a long time yet the task of social democracy is, instead of speculating on a great economic crash, "to organize the working classes politically and develop them as a democracy and to fight for all reforms in the state which are adapted to raise the working classes and transform the state in the direction of democracy."

Eduard Bernstein believed that socialist ideals could be achieved through evolution rather than revolution.

United Press International, Inc.

No one has questioned the necessity for the working classes to gain the control of government. The point at issue is between the theory of social cataclysm and the question whether with the given social development in Germany, and the present advanced state of its working classes in the towns and the country, a sudden catastrophe would be desirable in the interest of the social democracy. I have denied it and deny it again, because in my judgment a greater security for lasting success lies in a steady advance than in the possibilities offered by a catastrophic crash.

And, as I am firmly convinced that important periods in the development of nations cannot be leapt over, I lay the greatest value on the next tasks of social democracy, on the struggle for the political rights of the working man, on the political activity of working men in town and country for the interests of their class, as well as on the work of the industrial organization of the workers....

The conquest of political power by the working classes, the expropriation of capitalists, are no ends in themselves but only means for the accomplishment of certain aims and endeavours. As such they are demands in the program of social democracy and are not attacked by me. Nothing can be said beforehand as to the circumstances of their accomplishments; we can only fight for their realization. But the conquest of political power necessitates the possession of political *rights*; and the most important problem of tactics which German social democracy has at the present time to solve, appears to me to be to devise the best ways for the extension of the political and economic rights of the German working classes.

"Every legal constitution is the product *of a revolution. In the history of classes, revolution is the act of political creation."*

The Error of Evolutionary Socialism

Rosa Luxemburg

Rosa Luxemburg (1871-1919) was a Marxist revolutionary and one of the founders of the German Communist party. A contemporary of Eduard Bernstein, she earned a reputation for brilliance in party circles with her *Social Reform or Revolution?* in which she argued against Bernstein's revisionist theories. Her works, all of which echo many traditional Marxist ideas, include: *The Crisis in the German Social Democracy, Spartacus Letters,* and *The Accumulation of Capital.* Luxemburg was a fearless and tireless party worker who, despite being crippled and plagued with poor health, never avoided dangerous or compromising situations. Imprisoned in Poland from 1907 to 1914, she was murdered in 1919 in Berlin by a group of German soldiers. In the following viewpoint, she attempts to explain why Bernstein's parliamentary methods would prove counterproductive and favorable to the bourgeoisie.

As you read, consider the following questions:

1. Why does the author oppose legislative reform (democratic means) as a road to socialism?
2. According to the author, what distinguishes bourgeois society from other class societies?

Rosa Luxemburg, *Reform or Revolution?* New York: Pathfinder Press, 1973.

The fate of democracy is bound up, we have seen, with the fate of the labor movement. But does the development of democracy render superfluous or impossible a proletarian revolution, that is, the conquest of the political power by the workers?

Bernstein settles the question by weighing minutely the good and bad sides of social reform and social revolution. He does it almost in the same manner in which cinnamon or pepper is weighed out in a consumers' cooperative store. He sees the legislative course of historic development as the action of "intelligence," while the revolutionary course of historic development is for him the action of "feeling." Reformist activity, he recognizes as a slow method of historic progress, revolution as a rapid method of progress. In legislation he sees a methodic force; in revolution, a spontaneous force.

We have known for a long time that the petty-bourgeois reformer finds "good" and "bad" sides in everything. He nibbles a bit at all grasses. But the real course of events is little affected by such combinations. The carefully gathered little pile of the "good sides" of all things possible collapses at the first fillip of history. Historically, legislative reform and the revolutionary method function in accordance with influences that are much more profound than the consideration of the advantages or inconveniences of one method or another.

Legislation Favors the Bourgeoisie

In the history of bourgeois society, legislative reform served to strengthen progressively the rising class till the latter was sufficiently strong to seize political power, to suppress the existing juridical system, and to construct itself a new one. Bernstein, thundering against the conquest of political power as a theory of Blanquist violence, has the misfortune of labeling as a Blanquist error that which has always been the pivot and the motive force of human history. From the first appearance of class societies having the class struggle as the essential content of their history, the conquest of political power has been the aim of all rising classes. Here is the starting point and end of every historic period. This can be seen in the long struggle of the Latin peasantry against the financiers and nobility of ancient Rome, in the struggle of the medieval nobility against the bishops and in the struggle of the artisans against the nobles, in the cities of the Middle Ages. In more modern times, we see it in the struggle of the bourgeoisie against feudalism.

Legislative reform and revolution are not different methods of historic development that can be picked out at pleasure from the counter of history, just as one chooses hot or cold sausages. Legislative reform and revolution are different *factors* in the development of class society. They condition and complement each other, and are at the same time reciprocally exclusive, as are the north and south poles, the bourgeoisie and the proletariat.

Every legal constitution is the *product* of a revolution. In the history of classes, revolution is the act of political creation, while legislation is the political expression of the life of a society that has already come into being. Work for reform does not contain its own force, independent from revolution. During every historic period, work for reforms is carried on only in the direction given to it by the impetus of the last revolution and continues as long as the impulsion of the last revolution continues to make itself felt....

Superficial Cosmetic Change

People who pronounce themselves in favor of the method of legislative reform *in place of* and *in contradistinction to* the conquest of political power and social revolution, do not really choose a more tranquil, calmer, and slower road to the *same* goal, but a *different* goal. Instead of taking a stand for the establishment of a new society, they take a stand for surface modifications of the old society. If we follow the political conceptions of revisionism, we arrive at the same conclusion that is reached when we follow the economic theories of revisionism. Our program becomes not the realization of *socialism*, but the reform of *capitalism*; not the sup-

Half a century after her death, Rosa Luxemburg stirred new controversy when she appeared on a German postage stamp.

United Press International, Inc.

pression of the system of wage labor, but the diminution of exploitation, that is, the suppression of the abuses of capitalism instead of the suppression of capitalism itself.

Does the reciprocal role of legislative reform and revolution apply only to the class struggles of the past? Is it possible that now, as a result of the development of the bourgeois juridical system, the function of moving society from one historic phase to another belongs to legislative reform and that the conquest of state power by the proletariat has really become "an empty phrase," as Bernstein put it?

The very opposite is true. What distinguishes bourgeois society from other class societies, from ancient society and from the social order of the Middle Ages? Precisely the fact that class domination does not rest on "acquired rights" but on *real economic relations*—the fact that wage labor is not a juridical relation but purely an economic relation. In our juridical system, there is not a single legal formula for the class domination of today....

The Yoke of Capitalism

The situation is entirely different now. No law obliges the proletariat to submit itself to the yoke of capitalism. Poverty, the lack of means of production, obliges the proletariat to submit itself to the yoke of capitalism. And no law in the world can give to the proletariat the means of production while it remains in the framework of bourgeois society, for not laws but economic development have torn the means of production from the producers' possession....

It is one of the peculiarities of the capitalist order that within it all the elements of the future society first assume, in their development, a form not approaching socialism but, on the contrary, a form moving more and more away from socialism. Production takes on a progressively increasing social character. But under what form is the social character of capitalist production expressed? It is expressed in the form of the large enterprise, in the form of the shareholding concern, the cartel, within which the capitalist antagonisms, capitalist exploitation, the oppression of labor power are augmented to the extreme.

"The Fabian Society is perfectly constitutional in its attitude, and its methods are those usual in political life in England."

Socialism Through Democracy

Fabian Society

The Fabian Society was an English revisionist socialist group whose influence among socialists extended to continental Europe and abroad. It boasted an impressive list of luminaries as members including George Bernard Shaw, H.G. Wells, and Sidney and Beatrice Webb. The following viewpoint is an official statement published by the Society in 1896 that sets forth its aims and methods.

As you read, consider the following questions:

1. What is the aim of the Fabians?
2. What means do they advocate for achieving their goals?
3. How do the Fabians view Karl Marx?

George L. Mosse, et al, ed., *Europe in Review and Sources Since 1500*, Chicago: Rand McNally and Company, 1964. Also, *Full Report of the Proceedings of the International Workers' Congress, London, July and August, 1896*, London, 1896.

The object of the Fabian Society is to persuade the English people to make their political constitution thoroughly democratic and to socialise their industries sufficiently to make the livelihood of the people entirely independent of private Capitalism.

The Fabian Society endeavours to pursue its Socialist and Democratic objects with complete singleness of aim. For example:

It does not ask the English people to join the Fabian Society.

It does not propose that the practical steps towards Social-Democracy should be carried out by itself, or by any other specially organised Socialist society or party.

It brings all the pleasure and persuasion in its power to bear, not on the imaginary forces of the future, but on the existing forces of to-day, caring nothing by what name any party calls itself, or what principles, Socialist or other, it professes, but having regard solely to the tendency of its actions, supporting those which make for Socialism and Democracy, and opposing those which are reactionary....

The Fabian Society does not claim to be the people of England, or even the Socialist party, and therefore does not seek direct political representation by putting forward Fabian candidates at elections. But it loses no opportunity of influencing elections and inducing constituencies to select Socialists as their candidates. No person, however, can obtain the support of the Fabian Society, or escape its opposition, by merely repeating a few shibboleths and calling himself a Socialist or Social-Democrat....

English in Character

The Fabian Society is perfectly constitutional in its attitude, and its methods are those usual in political life in England.

The Fabian Society accepts the conditions imposed on it by human nature and by the national character and political circumstances of the English people. It sympathises with the ordinary man's preference for gradual, peaceful changes, to revolution, conflict with the army and police, and martyrdom. It recognises the fact that Social-Democracy is not the whole of the working-class programme, and that every separate measure towards the socialisation of industry will have to compete for precedence with numbers of other reforms. It therefore does not believe that the moment will ever come when the whole of Socialism will be staked on the issue of a single General Election or a single Bill in the House of Commons as between the proletariat on one side and the proprietariat on the other. Each installment of Social-Democracy will only be a measure among other measures, and will have to be kept to the front by an energetic Fabian section of the working-class party. The Fabian Society therefore begs those Socialists who are looking forward to a sensational historical crisis to join some other Society....

Socialism, as understood by the Fabian Society, means the organisation and conduct of the necessary industries of the country and the appropriation of all forms of economic rent of land and capital, by the nation as a whole, through the coordinate agency of the most suitable public authorities....

The Fabian Society strenuously maintains its freedom of thought and speech with regard to the errors of Socialist authors, economists, leaders, and parties, no less than to those of its opponents. It insists on the necessity of maintaining as critical an attitude towards Marx and Lassalle, some of whose views must by this time be discarded as erroneous or obsolete, as these eminent Socialists themselves maintained towards their predecessors, St. Simon and Robert Owen....

Playwright George Bernard Shaw, a famed member of the Fabian Society.

United Press International, Inc.

In view of the fact that the Socialist movement has been hitherto inspired, instructed, led, and suffered for by members of the middle class or "bourgeoisie," the Fabian Society, though not at all surprised to find these middle-class leaders attacking with much bitterness the narrow social ideals current in their own class, protests against the absurdity of Socialists representing the very class from which Socialism has sprung as specially hostile to it. The

Fabian Society has no romantic illusions as to the freedom of the proletariat from these same narrow ideals. Like all other Socialist societies, it can only educate the people in Socialism by making them conversant with the conclusions of the most enlightened members of the middle classes and their pupils. The Fabian Society therefore cannot reasonably use the words ''bourgeois'' or ''middle class'' as terms of reproach, more especially as it would thereby condemn a large proportion of its own members.

Light More Important than Heat

The Fabian Society endeavours to rouse social compunction by making the public conscious of the evil condition of society under the present system. This it does by the collection and publication of authentic and impartial statistical tracts, compiled, not from the works of Socialists, but from official sources. The first volume of Karl Marx's ''Das Kapital,'' which contains an immense mass of carefully verified facts concerning modern capitalistic civilisation, and practically nothing at all about Socialism, is probably the most successful propagandist work ever published. The Fabian Society, in its endeavours to continue the work of Marx in this direction, has found that the guesses made by Socialists at the condition of the people almost invariably flatter the existing system instead of, as might be suspected, exaggerating its evils. The Fabian Society therefore concluded that in the natural philosophy of Socialism, light is a more important factor than heat.

The Fabian Society is fully alive to the social value of what is called ''brain work,'' and deeply regrets that it cannot include under that description many of the speeches and articles produced at present in England either for or against Socialism....

Economic Reform

The Fabian Society does not put Socialism forward as a panacea for all the ills of human society, but only for those produced by defective organisation of industry and radically bad distribution of wealth.

The Fabian Society, by steadfastly refusing to sacrifice the interests of Socialism either to the mistakes of Socialists on the one hand, or the political convenience of the established political parties on the other, has been violently denounced from both sides, the Liberal and Socialist newspapers often vying with one another in their efforts to discredit the Fabian Society. The only compliments which the Fabian Society receives or expects from non-Fabian Socialists, are the applications for advice, speakers, and money, which are invariably made to it in all emergencies, and to which it always responds to the best of its ability.

"Socialism could not continue to exist without an apology for violence."

Socialism Through Violence

Georges Sorel

Syndicalism was a radical socialist movement, originating in France, which espoused control of the production and distribution of goods by federations of labor unions. Georges Sorel (1847-1922), a French social philosopher, was a leading spokesperson for the movement. Convinced that the evolutionary socialists were mere dupes of the industrial class, Sorel advocated the revolutionary seizure of industry and government by the workers. In the following viewpoint taken from his *Reflections on Violence* (1906), he supports the "general strike" as the most viable and potent weapon for achieving worker control.

As you read, consider the following questions:

1. In what ways does the Sorel viewpoint differ with the viewpoint by the Fabian Society?
2. How does the author propose that strikes be used to achieve a socialist order?

Georges Sorel, *Reflections on Violence*, London: George Allen & Unwin, Ltd., 1925. Reprinted with permission.

I do not hesitate to assert that Socialism could not continue to exist without an apology for violence.

It is in strikes that the proletariat asserts its existence. I cannot agree with the view which sees in strikes merely something analogous to the temporary rupture of commercial relations which is brought about when a grocer and the wholesale dealer from whom he buys his dried plums cannot agree about the price. The strike is a phenomenon of war. It is thus a serious misrepresentation to say that violence is an accident doomed to disappear from the strikes of the future.

The Language of Strikes

The social revolution is an extension of that war in which each great strike is an episode; this is the reason why Syndicalists speak of that revolution in the language of strikes; for them Socialism is reduced to the conception, the expectation of, and the preparation for the general strike, which, like the Napoleonic battle, is to completely annihilate a condemned *regime*....

The revolutionary Syndicates argue about Socialist action exactly in the same manner as military writers argue about war; they restrict the whole of Socialism to the general strike; they look upon every combination as one that should culminate in this catastrophe; they see in each strike a reduced facsimile, an essay, a preparation for the great final upheaval....

The English Workers

The possibility of the actual realisation of the general strike has been much discussed; it has been stated that the Socialist war could not be decided in one single battle. To the people who think themselves cautious, practical, and scientific the difficulty of setting great masses of the proletariat in motion at the same moment seems prodigious; they have analysed the difficulties of detail which such an enormous struggle would present. It is the opinion of the Socialist-sociologists, as also of the politicians, that the general strike is a popular dream, characteristic of the beginnings of a working-class movement; we have had quoted against us the authority of Sidney Webb [a Fabian socialist], who has decreed that the general strike is an illusion of youth, of which the English workers...soon rid themselves.

Socialism: A Class War

That the general strike is not popular in contemporary England, is a poor argument to bring against the historical significance of the idea, for the English are distinguished by an extraordinary lack of understanding of the class war...it is for England that the term *working-class aristocracy*, as a name for the trades unionists, was invented, and, as a matter of fact, trades unionism does pursue the acquisition of legal privileges. We might therefore say that the aversion felt by England for the general strike should be looked upon as strong presumptive evidence in favour of the latter by all those who look upon the class war as the essence of Socialism....

Socialism and Violence

It is to violence that Socialism owes those high ethical values by means of which it brings *salvation* to the modern world.

Georges Sorel, *Reflections on Violence*, 1925.

The conception of the general strike, engendered by the practice of violent strikes, admits the conception of an irrevocable overthrow. There is something terrifying in this which will appear more and more terrifying as violence takes a greater place in the mind of the proletariat.

*"The industry and commerce of the country...
were entrusted to a single syndicate representing
the people, to be conducted in the common
interest for the common profit."*

An Argument for Evolutionary Socialism

Edward Bellamy

Edward Bellamy (1850-1898) is perhaps best noted for his futuristic novel, *Looking Backward*. The following viewpoint is excerpted from this work, a utopian romance set in the year A.D. 2000. Julian West, the novel's hero, is a wealthy Bostonian living in the nineteenth century. A chronic insomniac, West would frequently have himself put to sleep by a hypnotist in an underground vault in his home. On one such occasion, his home burns to the ground and he survives without waking. He is discovered, still alive, in the year 2000 by a Dr. Leete who is excavating the site where West's home once stood. Leete explains to West that society has undergone a radical social and economic transformation as a result of a bloodless revolution in the 1890s. The viewpoint begins with Leete explaining to West the events which led to the revolution.

As you read, consider the following questions:

1. According to the author, what was happening to small businesses during the last decade of the century?
2. What eventually happened to the larger businesses and monopolies as portrayed by the author?
3. Were the social and economic changes that the author described violent?

Edward Bellamy, *Looking Backward, 2000-1887*. Boston: Houghton Mifflin Company, 1889.

''The records of the period show that the outcry against the concentration of capital was furious. Men believed that it threatened society with a form of tyranny more abhorrent than it had ever endured. They believed that the great corporations were preparing for them the yoke of a baser servitude than had ever been imposed on the race, servitude not to men but to soulless machines incapable of any motive but insatiable greed. Looking back, we cannot wonder at their desperation, for certainly humanity was never confronted with a fate more sordid and hideous than would have been the era of corporate tyranny which they anticipated.

Growth of Monopolies

''Meanwhile, without being in the smallest degree checked by the clamor against it, the absorption of business by ever larger monopolies continued. In the United States, where this tendency was later in developing than in Europe, there was not, after the beginning of the last quarter of the century, any opportunity whatever for individual enterprise in any important field of industry, unless backed by a great capital. During the last decade of the century, such small businesses as still remained were fast failing survivals of a past epoch, or mere parasites on the great corporations, or else existed in fields too small to attract the great capitalists. Small businesses, as far as they still remained, were reduced to the condition of rats and mice, living in holes and corners, and counting on evading notice for the enjoyment of existence. The railroads had gone on combining till a few great syndicates controlled every rail in the land. In manufactories, every important staple was controlled by a syndicate. These syndicates, pools, trusts, or whatever their name, fixed prices and crushed all competition except when combination as vast as themselves arose. Then a struggle, resulting in a still greater consolidation, ensued. The great city bazaar crushed its country rivals with branch stores, and in the city itself absorbed its smaller rivals till the business of a whole quarter was concentrated under one roof with a hundred former proprietors of shops serving as clerks. Having no business of his own to put his money in, the small capitalist, at the same time that he took service under the corporation, found no other investment for his money but its stocks and bonds, thus becoming doubly dependent upon it.

Increased Efficiency

''The fact that the desperate popular opposition to the consolidation of business in a few powerful hands had no effect to check it, proves that there must have been a strong economical reason for it. The small capitalists, with their innumerable petty concerns, had, in fact, yielded the field to the great aggregations of capital, because they belonged to a day of small things and were totally incompetent to the demands of an age of steam and telegraphs and the gigantic scale of its enterprises. To restore the former order of

67

things, even if possible, would have involved returning to the day of stage-coaches. Oppressive and intolerable as was the regime of the great consolidations of capital, even its victims, while they cursed it, were forced to admit the prodigious increase of efficiency which had been imparted to the national industries, the vast economies effected by concentration of management and unity of organization, and to confess that since the new system had taken the place of the old, the wealth of the world had increased at a rate before undreamed of. To be sure this vast increase had gone chiefly to make the rich richer, increasing the gap between them and the poor; but the fact remained that, as a means merely of producing wealth, capital had been proved efficient in proportion to its consolidation. The restoration of the old system with the subdivision of capital, if it were possible, might indeed bring back a greater equality of conditions with more individual dignity and freedom, but it would be at the price of general poverty and the arrest of material progress.

Freedom and Slavery

Our boasted freedom necessarily involves slavery, so long as we recognize private property in land. Until that is abolished, Declarations of Independence and Acts of Emancipation are in vain. So long as one man can claim the exclusive ownership of the land from which other men must live, slavery will exist, and as material progress goes on, must grow and deepen!

Henry George, *Progress and Poverty*, 1929.

"Was there, then, no way of commanding the services of the mighty wealth-producing principle of consolidated capital, without bowing down to a plutocracy like that of Carthage? As soon as men began to ask themselves these questions, they found the answer ready for them. The movement toward the conduct of business by larger and larger aggregations of capital, the tendency toward monopolies, which had been so desperately and vainly resisted, was recognized at last, in its true significance, as a process which only needed to complete its logical evolution to open a golden future to humanity.

The Evolution Is Completed

"Early in the last century the evolution was completed by the final consolidation of the entire capital of the nation. The industry and commerce of the country, ceasing to be conducted by a set of irresponsible corporations and syndicates of private persons at their caprice and for their profit, were entrusted to a single syndicate representing the people, to be conducted in the common interest for the common profit. The nation, that is to say, organized as the one great business corporation in which all other corporations were absorbed; it became the one capitalist in the place of all other capitalists, the sole employer, the final monopoly in which all previous and lesser monopolies were swallowed up, a monopoly in the profits and economies of which all citizens shared. In a word, the people of the United States concluded to assume the conduct of their own business, just as one hundred odd years before they had assumed the conduct of their own government, organizing now for industrial purposes on precisely the same grounds on which they had then organized for political ends. At last, strangely late in the world's history, the obvious fact was perceived that no business is so essentially the public business as the industry and commerce on which the people's livelihood depends, and that to entrust it to private persons to be managed for private profit, is a folly similar in kind, though vastly greater in magnitude, to that of surrendering the functions of political government to kings and nobles to be conducted for their personal glorification."

"Such a stupendous change as you describe," said I, "did not, of course, take place without great bloodshed and terrible convulsions."

A Bloodless Transition

"On the contrary," replied Dr. Leete, "there was absolutely no violence. The change had been long forseen. Public opinion had become fully ripe for it, and the whole mass of the people was behind it. There was no more possibility of opposing it by force than by argument. On the other hand the popular sentiment toward the great corporations and those identified with them had ceased to be one of bitterness, as they came to realize their necessity as a link, a transition phase, in the evolution of the true industrial system. The most violent foes of the great private monopolies were now forced to recognize how invaluable and indispensable had been their office in educating the people up to the point of assuming control of their own business. Fifty years before, the consolidation of the industries of the country under national control would have seemed a very daring experiment to the most sanguine. But by a series of object lessons, seen and studied by all men, the great corporations had taught the people an entirely new set of ideas on this subject. They had seen for many years syndicates handling revenues greater than those of states, and directing the labors of hundreds of thousands of men with an efficiency and economy unattainable in smaller operations. It had come to be recognized as an axiom that the larger the business the simpler the principles that can be applied to it; that, as the machine is truer than the hand, so the system, which in a great concern does the work of the master's eye in a small business, turns out more accurate results. Thus it came about that, thanks to the corporations themselves, when it was proposed that the nation should assume their functions, the suggestion implied nothing which seemed impracticable even to the timid. To be sure it was a step beyond any yet taken, a broader generalization, but the very fact that the nation would be the sole corporation in the field would, it was seen, relieve the undertaking of many difficulties with which the partial monopolies had contended."

"Socialism...implies organization; organization implies directing authority; and the one and the other are strict reflections of the revolutions undergone by the tool of production."

An Argument for Revolutionary Socialism

Daniel De Leon

Daniel De Leon (1852-1914), an American socialist leader, immigrated to the United States from the Spanish speaking island of Curacao. He was the Socialist Labor party's candidate for governor of New York in 1899. A doctrinaire Marxist revolutionary, he devoted his life to promulgating the violent overthrow of existing capitalistic society. The following viewpoint is taken from a speech De Leon delivered in 1896. In it, he offers his rationale for socialism through revolution.

As you read, consider the following questions:

1. Does the author believe that the "State" and "government" have always existed? What examples does he offer to support his beliefs?
2. Does the author believe that capitalism resulted from a revolution? Explain your answer.
3. According to the author, in what way does socialism differ from anarchism?

Daniel De Leon, *Socialist Landmarks*. Palo Alto, California: New York Labor News Company, 1952. Reprinted with permission.

Take...a poodle. You can reform him in a lot of ways. You can shave his whole body and leave a tassel at the tip of his tail; you may bore a hole through each ear, and tie a blue bow on one and a red bow on the other; you may put a brass collar around his neck with your initials on, and a trim little blanket on his back; yet, throughout, a poodle he was and a poodle he remains. Each of these changes probably wrought a corresponding change in the poodle's life....Each of these transformations or stages may mark a veritable epoch in the poodle's existence. And yet, essentially, a poodle he was, a poodle he is, and a poodle he will remain. That is *Reform*....

What, then, with an eye single upon the differences between *reform* and *revolution*, does Socialism mean? To point out that, I shall take up two or three of what I may style the principal nerve centers of the movement.

The State and Government

One of these principal nerve centers is the question of "government" or the question of the "State." How many of you have not seen upon the shelves of our libraries books on the "History of the State"; on the "Limitations of the State"; on "What the State Should Do, and What It Should Not Do"; on the "Legitimate Functions of the State," and so on into infinity? Nevertheless, there is not one among all of these, the products, as they all are, of the vulgar and superficial character of capitalist thought, that fathoms the question, or actually defines the "State." Not until we reach the great works of the American [Lewis H.] Morgan, of Marx and Engels, and of other Socialist philosophers, is the matter handled with that scientific lucidity that proceeds from facts, leads to sound conclusions, and breaks the way to practical work. Not until you know and understand the history of the "State" and of "government" will you understand one of the cardinal principles upon which Socialist organization rests, nor will you be in a condition to organize successfully....

We are told that "government" has always been as it is today, and always will be. This is the first fundamental error of what Karl Marx justly calls capitalistic vulgarity of thought....

Our Indian Ancestors

When man started on his career, after having got beyond the state of the savage, he realized that cooperation was a necessity to him. He understood that together with others he could face his enemies in a better way than alone; he could hunt, fish, fight more successfully. Following the instructions of the great writer Morgan...we look to the Indian communities, the Indian settlements, as a type of the social system that our ancestors, all of them, without exception, went through at some time.

The Indian lived in the community condition. The Indian lived under a system of common property....They cooperated, worked together, and they had a central directing authority among them....It makes no difference how that central directing authority was elected; there it was. But note this: its function was to direct the cooperative or collective efforts of the communities, and, in so doing, it shared actively in the productive work of the communities. Without its work, the work of the communities would not have been done.

Need for Revolution

The state is the product and the manifestation of the irreconcilability of class antagonisms. When, where , and to what extent the State arises, depends directly on when, where, and to what extent the class antagonisms of a given society cannot be objectively reconciled. And conversely the existence of the state proves that the class antagonisms are irreconcilable....

The substitution of a proletarian for the capitalist State is impossible without a violent revolution.

N. Lenin, *The State and Revolution*, 1919.

When, in the further development of society, the tools of production grew and developed—grew and developed beyond the point reached by the Indian; when the art of smelting iron ore was discovered; when thereby that leading social cataclysm, wrapped in the mists of ages, yet discernible, took place that rent former communal society in twain along the line of sex, the males being able, the females unable, to wield the tool of production—then society was cast into a new mold; the former community, with its democratic equality of rights and duties, vanishes, and a new system turned up, divided into two sections, the one able, the other unable, to work at production. The line that separated these two sections, being at first the line of sex, could, in the very nature of things, not yet be sharp or deep. Yet, notwithstanding, in the very shaping of these two sections—one able, the other unable, to feed itself—we have the first premonition of *classes*, of class distinctions, of the division of society into the *independent* and the *dependent*, into *master* and *slaves, ruler* and *ruled.*

Revolutionary Changes

Simultaneously, with this revolution, we find the first changes in the nature of the central directing authority, of that body whose original function was to share in, by directing, production. Just as soon as economic equality is destroyed, and the economic classes crop up in society, the functions of the central directing authority gradually begin to change, until finally, when, after a long range of years, moving slowly at first, and then with the present hurricane velocity under capitalism proper, the tool has developed further, and further, and still further, and has reached its present fabulous perfection and magnitude; when, through its private ownership the tool has wrought a revolution within a revolution by dividing society, no longer along the line of sex, but strictly along the line of ownership or non-ownership of the land on and the tool with which to work; when the privately owned, mammoth tool of today has reduced more than fifty-two percent of our population to the state of being utterly unable to feed without first selling themselves into wage slavery, while it, at the same time, saps the ground from under about thirty-nine percent of our people, the middle class, whose puny tools, small capital, render them certain victims of competition with the large capitalists, and makes them desperate; when the economic law that asserts itself under the system of private ownership of the tool has concentrated these private owners into about eight percent of the nation's inhabitants, has thereby enabled this small capitalist class to live without toil, and to compel the majority, the class of the proletariat, to toil without living; when, finally, it has come to the pass in which our country now finds itself, that, as was stated in Congress, ninety-four percent of the taxes are spent in "protecting property"—the property of the trivially small capitalist class—and not in protecting life, when, in short, the privately owned tool has wrought this work, and the classes—the idle rich and the working poor—are in full bloom—then the central directing authority of old stands transformed; its pristine functions of aiding in, by directing, production have been supplanted by the functions of holding down the dependent, the slave, the ruled, i.e., the working class. Then, and not before, lo, the States, the modern State, the capitalist State! Then, lo, the government, the modern government, the capitalist government—equipped mainly, if not solely, with the means of suppression, of oppression, of tyranny!

Anarchism and Socialism

In sight of these manifestations of the modern State, the Anarchist—the rose-water and the dirty-water variety alike—shouts: "Away with all central directing authority; see what it does; it can only do mischief; it always did mischief!" But Socialism is not anarchy. Socialism does not, like the chicken in the fable, just out of the shell, start with the knowledge of that day. Socialism rejects the premises and the conclusions of anarchy upon the State and upon government. What Socialism says is: "Away with the economic system that alters the beneficient functions of the central directing authority from an aid to production into a means of oppression." And it proceeds to show that, when the instruments of production shall be owned, no longer by the minority, but shall be restored to the Commonwealth [the useful producers]; that when, as a result of this, no longer the minority or any portion of the people shall be in poverty, and classes, class distinctions and class rule shall, as they necessarily must, have vanished, that then the central directing authority will lose all its repressive functions, and is bound to reassume the functions it had in the old communities of our ancestors, become again a necessary aid, and assist in production....

Interdependence of Society

Our system of production is in the nature of an orchestra. No one man, no one town, no one State, can be said any longer to be independent of the others; the whole people of the United States, every individual therein, is dependent and interdependent upon all the others. The nature of the machinery of production; the subdivision of labor, which aids cooperation, and which cooperation fosters, and which is necessary to the plentifulness of production that civilization requires, compel a harmonious working together of all departments of labor, and thence compel the establishment of a central directing authority, of an orchestral director, so to speak, of the orchestra of the Cooperative Commonwealth.

Such is the State or government that the Socialist revolution carries in its womb. Today, production is left to anarchy, and only tyranny, the twin sister of anarchy, is organized.

Socialism, accordingly, implies organization; organization implies directing authority; and the one and the other are strict reflections of the revolutions undergone by the tool of production. Reform, on the other hand, skims the surface, and with "referendums" and similar devices limits itself to external tinkerings.

Understanding Words
in Context

Readers occasionally come across words which they do not recognize. And frequently, because they do not know a word or words, they will not fully understand the passage being read. Obviously, the reader can look up an unfamiliar word in a dictionary. However, by carefully examining the word in the context in which it is used, the word's meaning can often be determined. A careful reader may find clues to the meaning of the word in surrounding words, ideas, and attitudes.

Below are excerpts from the viewpoints in this chapter. In each excerpt, one or two words are printed in italics. Try to determine the meaning of each word by reading the excerpt. Under each excerpt you will find four definitions for the italicized word. Choose the one that is closest to your understanding of the word.

Finally, use a dictionary to see how well you have understood the words in context. It will be helpful to discuss with others the clues which helped you decide on each word's meaning.

1. To the people who think themselves cautious, practical, and scientific, the difficulty of setting great masses of the proletariat in motion seems *PRODIGIOUS*.

   PRODIGIOUS means:
   a) trivial
   b) exaggerated
   c) forbidding
   d) unrealistic

2. The carefully gathered pile of all good things collapses at the first *FILLIP* of history.

   FILLIP means:
   a) sharp blow
   b) mention
   c) interpretation
   d) description

76

3. When formerly communal societies were divided along the line of sex, we have the first *PREMONITION* of class distinctions.

   PREMONITION means:
   a) foreshadowing
   b) reaction
   c) difference
   d) understanding

4. No person can obtain the support of the Fabian Society by merely repeating a few *SHIBBOLETHS* and calling himself a socialist.

   SHIBBOLETHS means:
   a) experiences
   b) slogans
   c) questions
   d) scare tactics

5. Strikes are not *ANALOGOUS* to the temporary rupture of commercial relations when a grocer and a wholesale dealer cannot agree about price.

   ANALOGOUS means:
   a) necessary
   b) indifferent
   c) harmful
   d) similar

6. Does the development of democracy make *SUPERFLUOUS* the conquest of political power by the workers?

   SUPERFLUOUS means:
   a) unusual
   b) unnecessary
   c) slow
   d) possible

7. Fifty years before, the consolidation of the industries under national control would have seemed a very daring experiment to the most *SANGUINE*.
   SANGUINE means:
   a) boring
   b) optimistic
   c) unique
   d) risky

8. The Fabian Society does not put socialism forward as a *PANACEA* for all the ills of human society.

   PANACEA means:
   a) cure-all
   b) requirement
   c) disguise
   d) distraction

Bibliography

The following bibliography deals with the subject matter of this chapter.

Edward Bellamy	*Equality.* New York: Appleton and Co., 1897.
Eduard Bernstein	*Cromwell and Communism: Socialism and Democracy in the Great English Revolution.* London: G. Allen and Unwin, 1930.
Nikolai Bukharin	*Selected Writings on the State and the Transition to Socialism.* Armonk, NY: M.E. Sharpe, 1902.
George D.H. Cole	*Fabian Socialism.* London: G. Allen and Unwin, 1943.
Daniel De Leon	"The Historic Side of Expansion," *The People,* May 25, 1985.
Fabian Society	*The Administrators: The Reform of Civil Service by a Fabian Group.* London: Fabian Society, 1964.
Peter Gay	*The Dilemma of Democratic Socialism: Eduard Bernstein's Challenge to Marx.* New York: Octagon, 1979.
Albert S. Lindeman	*A History of European Socialism.* New Haven, CT: Yale University Press, 1984.
Arthur Lipow	*Authoritarian Socialism in America: Edward Bellamy and the Nationalist Movement.* Berkeley: University of California Press, 1982.
Rosa Luxemburg	*The Accumulation of Capital.* New York: Modern Reader Paperbacks, 1968.
Rosa Luxemburg	*The Russian Revolution: Leninism or Marxism?* Ann Arbor: University of Michigan Press, 1961.
The People	"De Leon and the Socialist Movement," June 9, 1984.
Jonathan Ree	*Proletarian Philosophers: Problems in Socialist Culture in Britain, 1900-1940.* New York: Oxford University Press, 1894.
Georges Sorel	*Essays in Socialism and Philosophy.* New York: Oxford University Press, 1976.

Socialism and Welfare

Introduction

When Franklin D. Roosevelt was elected president in 1932, the United States was in the midst of the Great Depression. An aura of despair enveloped the country as chronic unemployment (peaking at an unprecedented 36 percent), large and small business failures, and the collapse of the countless savings institutions spread with epidemic swiftness and virulence. The economic situation kept spiraling downward creating a vicious cycle. As more and more businesses failed or declined, the ranks of the

A typical depression scene: Unemployed men waiting in line for a meal.

unemployed and needy grew. To combat the menace and provide a psychological bolster to a disheartened nation, Roosevelt, in his inaugural address, offered his fellow citizens a "New Deal." The "New Deal" was to do more than revitalize the sick economy. It promised to infuse the entire economic system with a social conscience.

"The money changers," he said, "have fled from their high seats in the temple of our civilization. We may now restore that temple to the ancient truths. The measure of the restoration lies in the extent to which we apply social values more noble than mere monetary profit." Roosevelt subsequently converted these words into deeds by successfully guiding through congress a host of economic and social welfare legislation. This legislation not only succeeded in providing employment and other forms of economic relief, but it also set in motion an innovative and irreversible trend in American society. By using federal or public funds to finance the welfare needs of the people, the government was involving itself in areas which previously were the preserve of the private sector of the economy.

At the time of Roosevelt's first administration, the theory and

practice of welfare were not new in the United States. Greatly influenced by European reformers, many Americans, toward the end of the nineteenth century, were providing relief to unemployed and low income families in slum and devastated areas throughout the country. Jane Addams' Hull House in Chicago, the Salvation Army, and the American Red Cross were just some of the numerous agencies dedicated to this task. Even Andrew Carnegie, America's premiere industrialist and defender of the capitalistic system, believed it was his duty to channel many of his millions into charitable foundations. Yet the "New Deal" took America beyond these earlier instances of private philanthropy. For the first time on so large a scale, the government took it upon itself to oversee the welfare needs of the country. By way of government dole or subsidized work projects, every taxpayer, like it or not, was contributing to the economic relief of the nation's needy.

Many claimed that the "New Deal" was cutting into the very heart of the free enterprise system in the United States. They saw it as a form of "creeping socialism" which, in time, would totally undermine the work ethic crucial to the success of capitalism. The end result would be the establishment of a "welfare state" in which most or all social and economic services would be dealt with by the government. However, supporters of the "New Deal" were convinced that there was no alternative. Private funds were obviously not relieving the economic plight of the nation and therefore it was the moral duty of government to act decisively.

With the arrival of World War II and the general prosperity which followed it, the "New Deal" was laid to rest. Yet the debate regarding welfarism continues. The present chapter, beginning with Roosevelt's first inaugural address, includes a wide range of arguments for and against government welfare. While reading them, it would be useful to consider the following questions. Are there any conditions under which welfare seems absolutely necessary? Does welfare rob people of the incentive to work? Must welfare inevitably lead to state socialism or can it be made to harmonize with capitalism?

"[Putting people to work] can be accomplished in part by direct recruiting by the Government itself."

The Depression and Government Help

Franklin D. Roosevelt

Franklin D. Roosevelt (1882-1945) began his political career in 1910 as a senator from New York. He resigned his senate seat in 1913 to join Woodrow Wilson's administration as assistant secretary of the Navy. He was the unsuccessful democratic vice presidential candidate in the 1920 national elections. Stricken with paralytic polio in 1921, Roosevelt never recovered the use of his legs. Despite his infirmity, however, he reentered politics in 1929 and was elected governor of New York. In 1932, while serving his second term as governor, he was elected president of the United States. In the following viewpoint from his first inaugural address, Roosevelt stresses the need for government intervention to overcome the economic miseries brought on by the Great Depression.

As you read, consider the following questions:

1. What are some of the troubles Roosevelt describes?
2. What role does he believe the government should play?

Samuel I. Rosenman, editor, *The Public Papers and Addresses of Franklin D. Roosevelt,* Volume I, New York: Random House, 1938.

I am certain that my fellow Americans expect that on my induction into the Presidency I will address them with a candor and a decision which the present situation of our nation impels. This is pre-eminently the time to speak the truth, the whole truth, frankly and boldly. Nor need we shrink from honestly facing conditions in our country today. This great nation will endure as it has endured, will revive and will prosper. So, first of all, let me assert my firm belief that the only thing we have to fear is fear itself—nameless, unreasoning, unjustified terror which paralyzes needed efforts to convert retreat into advance. In every dark hour of our national life a leadership of frankness and vigor has met with that understanding and support of the people themselves which is essential to victory. I am convinced that you will again give that support to leadership in these critical days.

Troubled Times

In such a spirit on my part and on yours we face our common difficulties. They concern, thank God, only material things. Values have shrunken to fantastic levels; taxes have risen; our ability to pay has fallen; government of all kinds is faced by serious curtailment of income; the means of exchange are frozen in the currents of trade; the withered leaves of industrial enterprise lie on every side; farmers find no markets for their produce; the savings of many years in thousands of families are gone.

More important, a host of unemployed citizens face the grim problem of existence, and an equally great number toil with little return. Only a foolish optimist can deny the dark realities of the moment....

The Creation of Jobs

Our greatest primary task is to put people to work. This is no unsolvable problem if we face it wisely and courageously. It can be accomplished in part by direct recruiting by the Government itself, treating the task as we would treat the emergency of a war, but at the same time, through this employment, accomplishing greatly needed projects to stimulate and reorganize the use of our natural resources.

Hand in hand with this, we must frankly recognize the over-balance of population in our industrial centers and, by engaging on a national scale in a redistribution, endeavor to provide a better use of the land for those best fitted for the land. The task can be helped by definite efforts to raise the values of agricultural products and with this the power to purchase the output of our cities. It can be helped by preventing realistically the tragedy of the growing loss through foreclosure of our small homes and our farms. It can be helped by insistence that the Federal, State and local governments act forthwith on the demand that their cost be drastically reduced. It can be helped by the unifying of relief activities which today are often scattered, uneconomical and unequal. It can be helped by national planning for and supervision of all forms of transportation and of communications and other utilities which have a definitely public character. There are many ways in which it can be helped, but it can never be helped merely by talking about it. We must act, and act quickly.

Facing a Crisis

In the spring of 1933, we faced a crisis....We were against revolution. And, therefore, we waged war against those conditions which make revolution—against the inequalities and resentments that breed them.

Franklin D. Roosevelt, Democratic State Convention, New York, September 30, 1936.

Finally, in our progress toward a resumption of work we require two safeguards against a return of the evils of the old order: there must be a strict supervision of all banking and credits and investments, there must be an end to speculation with other people's money; and there must be provision for an adequate but sound currency.

These are the lines of attack. I shall presently urge upon a new Congress in special session, detailed measures for their fulfillment, and I shall seek the immediate assistance of the several States.

"*The friendliness and charity of our countrymen can always be relied upon to relieve their fellow-citizens in misfortune.*"

The Depression and Private Generosity

Herbert C. Hoover

Herbert C. Hoover (1874-1964) was secretary of commerce during the administrations of Warren G. Harding and Calvin Coolidge before being elected president of the United States in 1928. It was during his first year in office that the depression began. A staunch defender of a "free economy," Hoover was convinced that governmental interference in the nation's economic affairs would eventually erode the political freedom Americans enjoyed. He therefore advocated private generosity as a means to deal with the economic crisis. Although Hoover never totally ruled out the use of government programs and funds, he firmly believed that individual and group charity would resolve the situation. The following viewpoint is part of a press statement issued in February 1931 reaffirming his principles.

As you read, consider the following questions:

1. Why does Hoover oppose government aid for the poor?
2. What experience does he have with the problems of poverty?

William Starr Myers, editor, *The State Papers and Other Public Writings of Herbert Hoover*, New York: Doubleday, Doran & Co., 1934. Reprinted with permission.

Certain senators have issued a public statement to the effect that unless the President and the House of Representatives agree to appropriations from the Federal Treasury for charitable purposes they will force an extra session of Congress.

I do not wish to add acrimony to a discussion, but would rather state this case as I see its fundamentals.

Private Versus Public Help

This is not an issue as to whether people shall go hungry or cold in the United States. It is solely a question of the best method by which hunger and cold shall be prevented. It is a question as to whether the American people on one hand will maintain the spirit of charity and mutual self help through voluntary giving and the responsibility of local government as distinguished on the other hand from appropriations out of the Federal Treasury for such purposes. My own conviction is strongly that if we break down this sense of responsibility of individual generosity to individual and mutual self help in the country in times of national difficulty and if we start appropriations of this character we have not only impaired something infinitely valuable in the life of the American people but have struck at the roots of self-government. Once this has happened it is not the cost of a few score millions but we are faced with the abyss of reliance in the future upon Government charity in some form or other. The money involved is indeed the least of the costs to American ideals and American institutions.

President Cleveland, in 1887, confronted with a similar issue stated in part:

> A prevalent tendency to disregard the limited mission of this power and duty should, I think, be steadfastly resisted, to the end that the lesson should be constantly enforced that though the people support the Government, the Government should not support the people.
>
> The friendliness and charity of our countrymen can always be relied upon to relieve their fellow-citizens in misfortune. This has been repeatedly and quite lately demonstrated. Federal aid in such cases encourages the expectation of paternal care on the part of the Government and weakens the sturdiness of our national character, while it prevents the indulgence among our people of that kindly sentiment and conduct which strengthens the bonds of a common brotherhood.

Role of Relief Agencies

And there is a practical problem in all this. The help being daily extended by neighbors, by local and national agencies, by municipalities, by industry and a great multitude of organizations throughout the country today is many times any appropriation yet proposed. The opening of the doors of the Federal Treasury is likely to stifle this giving and thus destroy far more resources than the proposed charity from the Federal Government.

Herbert Hoover's policies of government nonintervention failed to lift the country out of the Great Depression.

The basis of successful relief in national distress is to mobilize and organize the infinite number of agencies of self help in the community. That has been the American way of relieving distress among our own people and the country is successfully meeting its problem in the American way today.

We have two entirely separate and distinct situations in the country; the first is the drought area; the second is the unemployment in our large industrial centers—for both of which these appropriations attempt to make charitable contributions....

Our American System

Our American system requires that municipal, county and state governments shall use their own resources and credit before seeking such assistance from the Federal Treasury.

I have indeed spent much of my life in fighting hardship and starvation both abroad and in the southern states. I do not feel that I should be charged with lack of human sympathy for those who suffer but I recall that in all the organizations with which I have been connected over these many years, the foundation has been to summon the maximum of self help. I am proud to have sought the help of Congress in the past for nations who were so disorganized by war and anarchy that self help was impossible. But even these appropriations were but a tithe of that which was coincidently mobilized from the public charity of the United States and foreign countries. There is no such paralysis in the United States and I am confident that our people have the resources, the initiative, the courage, the stamina and kindliness of spirit to meet this situation in the way they have met their problems over generations.

"Public services have, to use the economist's word, a strong redistributional effect."

The Advantages of Public Welfare

John Kenneth Galbraith

A native of Canada, John Kenneth Galbraith is a highly respected economist who served as an economic advisor to presidents Kennedy and Johnson. He was the United States ambassador to India (1961-1963) and national chairman of Americans for Democratic Action (1967). A prolific author, Galbraith is an economic liberal who advocates a limited form of capitalism. In the following viewpoint, he attempts to explain the conditions under which government economic intervention is not only necessary, but also morally imperative.

As you read, consider the following questions:

1. According to the author, what causes poverty?
2. What do "modern conservatives" think, according to the author?
3. How does the author believe that poverty can be eliminated?

John Kenneth Galbraith, "Let Us Begin: An Invitation to Action on Poverty," *Harper's Magazine*. March 1964. Reprinted with permission. Copyright © 1964 by *Harper's Magazine*.

The problem of poverty in the United States is the problem of people who for reasons of location, education, health, environment in youth or mental deficiency, or race are not able to participate effectively—or at all—in the economic life of the nation. Being barred from participation they are denied the income that accrues to participants. So they live in deprivation.

Those who argue that a steady expansion in economic output is a necessary condition for the elimination of poverty have a valid case. People who are able to participate in the economy must have a chance for jobs. And there also continues to be good reason for seeking a broad and equitable distribution of the revenues from production. Despite considerable propaganda to the contrary, our greatest current need is not a decision to be tender to the well-to-do. Their situation is not nearly so desperate as popularly represented or the current Congressional desire to help the higher tax brackets would seem to suggest. We should continue to bear in mind that one makes an economy work not by rewarding the rich but by rewarding all who contribute to its success.

The Problem of Poverty

But on one elementary point there must be no doubt. If the head of a family is stranded deep on the Cumberland Plateau, or if he never went to school, or if he has no useful skill, or if his health is broken, or if he succumbed as a youngster to a slum environment, or if opportunity is denied to him because he is a Negro, then he will be poor and his family will be poor and that will be true no matter how opulent everyone else becomes. A very large part of the very worst poverty is the affliction of people who are unable to make a useful contribution to the economy. Being unable to contribute they receive nothing. They will continue to receive nothing no matter how rapidly the economy expands.

Equally there must be no doubt that the means for rescuing these people or their children—investment to conserve and develop resources, assistance in relocation of workers, assistance to new industries, vastly improved education, training and retraining, medical and mental care, youth employment, counseling, urban recreational facilities, housing, slum abatement, and the assurance of full civic equality—will require public effort and public funds. This must be honest effort and not pilot projects which are a modern device for simulating action without spending money. Poverty can be made to disappear. It won't be accomplished simply by stepping up the growth rate any more than it will be accomplished by incantation or ritualistic washing of the feet. Growth is only for those who can take advantage of it.

We have, of course, no hope of erasing this blot on our social life if we are affected by the thinking of that new and interesting cult which call themselves the modern conservatives. As to this, I suppose, there will be general agreement. The modern conservative is not even especially modern. He is engaged, on the contrary, in one of man's oldest, best financed, most applauded, and, on the whole, least successful exercises in moral philosophy. That is the search for a superior moral justification for selfishness. It is an exercise which always involves a certain number of internal contradictions and even a few absurdities. The conspicuously wealthy turn up urging the character-building value of privation for the poor....

Public Service

The quarrel is with those who see in sound public service some danger to society. In fact the public services are one of the two great forces in the fiscal system working for economic equity and social stability.

John Kenneth Galbraith.

It is the poor who need parks and whose children need swimming pools. Only the poor live in the slums and require the myriad of services that, we may hope, will one day mitigate urban congestion and public squalor. The well-to-do live in communities that have good schools; it is the schools of slum dwellers and wage and salary workers which would be principally improved by federal aid to education. Colleges and universities are more accessible to the rich than to the poor. It is the masses and not the classes who use mass transportation.

The elderly couple of less than average income would be the major beneficiary of medicare. Social security, minimum-wages enforcement, youth employment are all most important for the least well-to-do. It is poor children who play in dirty streets. It is their father who gets laid off when public works are suddenly cut back....

Public services have, to use the economist's word, a strong redistributional effect. And this effect is strongly in favor of those with lower incomes. Those who clamor the loudest for public economy are those for whom public services do the least. Tax reduction that curtails or limits public services has a double effect in comforting the comfortable and afflicting the poor.

This is something which liberals should not forget....

An Educational Approach

My impression is that poverty will be eliminated primarily by energetic action along lines on which we are already working—on civil rights, education, slum abatement, the rest....

To the best of knowledge there is no place in the world where a well-educated population is really poor. If so, let us here in the United States select, beginning next year, the hundred lowest-income counties (or, in the case of urban slums, more limited areas of substantial population and special need) and designate them as special educational districts. These would be equipped (or re-equipped) with a truly excellent and comprehensive school plant, including both primary and secondary schools, transportation, and the best in recreational facilities. The employment on construction in this part of the task would be well-adjusted to the areas of unemployment.

Next, in the manner of the Peace Corps, but with ample pay, an elite body of teachers would be assembled—ready to serve in the most remote areas, tough enough and well-trained enough to take on the worst slums, proud to go to Harlan County or to Harlem. By this one step we would overcome the present difficulty in getting good teachers to go where they are most needed....

Additional Help

Finally, the scheme should include modest educational grants to families to feed and clothe children for school and to compensate for their earnings. Breakfast should be available for children who need it in addition to lunch. Perhaps there should be an issue of efficient and attractive clothing. Specifically qualified members of the Corps would be available for counseling on home conditions, following up on truancy and delinquency, and otherwise insuring that these youngsters overcome the environment to which the accident of birth committed them. Those who need it would be provided with medical and psychiatric care. The year following, the program would be enlarged and extended to the next 150 or two hundred most abysmal areas. It would come to cover as quickly as possible the areas of need. But it would not go beyond areas of low income or, as in the case of the slums, of special educational problems.

This is not federal aid to education. It is an attack on poverty by what I would judge to be the most effective single step that could be taken. Can anyone argue that youngsters with these facilities and this training would share the dismal fate of their parents? As incomes rise above a specified level, the schools would be returned to the localities in accordance with a cost-sharing formula that would take account of increasing ability to pay. Those who fear federal control of education are amply protected. The effort would not affect them.

"The effect of Welfarism on freedom will be felt later on—after its beneficiaries have become its victims."

The Evils of Public Welfare

Barry Goldwater

The name Barry Goldwater and contemporary American conservatism are synonymous. The Republican party candidate for president in 1964 and a senator from Arizona, Goldwater has been a champion of the free enterprise system throughout his long public career. He essentially holds that government intervention in the economic life of a nation is an assault upon individual liberty. In the following viewpoint from his popular book *The Conscience of a Conservative*, he depicts governmental welfare as a form of creeping socialism which is harmful to both donor and recipient.

As you read, consider the following questions:

1. How, according to the author, has the strategy of the collectivists changed?
2. In the opinion of the author, does the "rhetoric of humanitarianism" promote welfarism?
3. What does the author believe are the consequences of welfarism?

Barry Goldwater, *The Conscience of a Conservative*, South Bend, IN: Victor Publishing Co., 1960. Reprinted with permission.

For many years it appeared that the principal domestic threat to our freedom was contained in the doctrines of Karl Marx. The collectivists—non-Communists as well as Communists—had adopted the Marxist objective of "socializing the means of production." And so it seemed that if collectivization were imposed, it would take the form of a State owned and operated economy. I doubt whether this is the main threat any longer.

The "Old" Threat

The collectivists have found, both in this country and in other industrialized nations of the West, that free enterprise has removed the economic and social conditions that might have made a class struggle possible. Mammoth productivity, wide distribution of wealth, high standards of living, the trade union movement—these and other factors have eliminated whatever incentive there might have been for the "proletariat" to rise up, peaceably or otherwise, and assume direct ownership of productive property. Significantly, the bankruptcy of doctrinaire Marxism has been expressly acknowledged by the Socialist Party of West Germany, and by the dominant faction of the Socialist Party of Great Britain. In this country the abandonment of the Marxist approach (outside the Communist Party, of course) is attested to by the negligible strength of the Socialist Party, and more tellingly perhaps, by the content of left wing literature and by the programs of left wing political organizations such as the Americans for Democratic Action.

The "New" Threat

The currently favored instrument of collectivization is the Welfare State. The collectivists have not abandoned their ultimate goal—to subordinate the individual to the State—but their strategy has changed. They have learned that Socialism can be achieved through Welfarism quite as well as through Nationalization. They understand that private property can be confiscated as effectively by taxation as by expropriating it. They understand that the individual can be put at the mercy of the State—not only by making the State his employer—but by divesting him of the means to provide for his personal needs and by giving the State the responsibility of caring for those needs from cradle to grave. Moreover, they have discovered—and here is the critical point—that *Welfarism is much more compatible with the political processes of a democratic society.* Nationalization ran into popular opposition, but the collectivists feel sure the Welfare State can be erected by the simple expedient of buying votes with promises of "free" federal benefits—"free" housing, "free" school aid, "free" hospitalization, "free" retirement pay and so on....The correctness of this estimate can be seen from the portion of the federal budget that is now allocated to welfare, an amount second only to the cost of national defense.

I do not welcome this shift of strategy. Socialism-through-

95

Welfarism poses a far greater danger to freedom than Socialism-through-Nationalization precisely because it *is* more difficult to combat. The evils of Nationalization are self-evident and immediate. Those of Welfarism are veiled and tend to be postponed. People can understand the consequences of turning over ownership of the steel industry, say, to the State; and they can be counted on to oppose such a proposal. But let the government increase its contribution to the "Public Assistance" program and we will, at most, grumble about excessive government spending. The effect of Welfarism on freedom will be felt later on—after its beneficiaries have become its victims, after dependence on government has turned into bondage and it is too late to unlock the jail.

But a far more important factor is Welfarism's strong emotional appeal to many voters, and the consequent temptations it presents the average politician. It is hard, as we have seen, to make out a case for State ownership. It is very different with the rhetoric of humanitarianism. How easy it is to reach the voters with earnest importunities for helping the needy. And how difficult for Conservatives to resist these demands without appearing to be callous and contemptuous of the plight of less fortunate citizens. Here, perhaps,

BEAST OF BURDEN

McElhattan from The American Way Features.

is the best illustration of the failure of the Conservative demonstration.

I know, for I have heard the questions often. Have you no sense of social obligation? the Liberals ask. Have you no concern for people who are out of work? for sick people who lack medical care? for children in overcrowded schools? Are you unmoved by the problems of the aged and disabled? Are you *against* human welfare?

Economic Control

Economic control is not merely control of a sector of human life which can be separated from the rest; it is the control of the means for all our ends.

Friedrich von Hayek, *The Road to Serfdom.*

The answer to all of these questions is, of course, no. But a simple "no" is not enough. I feel certain that Conservatism is through unless Conservatives can demonstrate and communicate the difference between being concerned with these problems and believing that the federal government is the proper agent for their solution.

The long range political consequences of Welfarism are plain enough: as we have seen, the State that is able to deal with its citizens as wards and dependents has gathered unto itself unlimited political and economic power and is thus able to rule as absolutely as any oriental despot....

Private Philanthropy

Let us, then, not blunt the noble impulses of mankind by reducing charity to a mechanical operation of the federal government. Let us, by all means, encourage those who are fortunate and able to care for the needs of those who are unfortunate and disabled. But let us do this in a way that is conducive to the spiritual as well as the material well-being of our citizens—and in a way that will preserve their freedom. Let welfare be a private concern. Let it be promoted by individuals and families, by churches, private hospitals, religious service organizations, community charities and other institutions that have been established for this purpose. If the objection is raised that private institutions lack sufficient funds, let us remember that every penny the federal government does *not* appropriate for welfare is potentially available for private use—and without the overhead charge for processing the money through the federal bureaucracy. Indeed, high taxes, for which government Welfarism is so largely responsible, is the biggest obstacle to fundraising by private charities.

> *"You have to recognize that on many important aspects of life things got worse for the poor, starting precisely when we kicked into high gear in the effort to help these people."*

Government Programs Undermine the Poor

Charles Murray, interviewed by *Reason*

Charles Murray reached almost instant national recognition with the publication of his book *Losing Ground*. In the following viewpoint, taken from an interview in which he discusses his book, Mr. Murray documents the failure of social welfare programs, claiming they reward the least industrious of the poor while punishing the most industrious. Social welfare programs, he contends, have virtually destroyed personal incentive and dignity and should be scrapped. Mr. Murray is senior research fellow at the Manhattan Institute for Policy Research. Formerly, he was chief scientist at the American Institutes for Research in Washington, DC.

As you read, consider the following questions:

1. The author gives a hypothetical case of a low-income couple whose lives become complicated with an unwanted pregnancy. How does the availability of welfare decide the outcome of their situation?
2. Why does Mr. Murray believe that welfare programs reward the least industrious poor?

Reason: Your book *Losing Ground* is very hot....Why did you go into this analysis of social welfare policy?

Murray: My professional background consisted of evaluating specific programs the government was sponsoring in education or social services or, when I was in Thailand, rural development. So few programs accomplished anything like their ambitions, despite a lot of effort, and I just kept seeing patterns and reasons why they didn't accomplish what they were supposed to accomplish, and that led to the spin-off.

Reason: I'd like to go into some detail about the conclusions of your book. You spend a lot of time looking at three points—1950, 1965, and 1980—in your trend analysis. Could you briefly summarize your findings there?

Murray: There are separate chapters in the book on poverty as officially measured, unemployment, wages, occupations, education, crime, and the family. In one of these areas, namely, wages and occupations among those who have jobs, I paint a very positive portrait of blacks with jobs getting white-collar work, which they had not done before, and achieving in effect wage parity for equivalent years of education and experience. But with that single exception, the trend lines show sudden and mysterious changes for the worse, mostly in the mid-1960s. In some cases you actually had advances turn into retreat. I would argue that in education, for example, we had been seeing marked improvements for minorities and poor people up through about 1964 and suddenly that just flipped. Similarly, there is a lot of evidence that among poor people—again, especially blacks—crime had been getting lower in the 1950s and that then there was a surging rise in the 1960s. Summarizing the data, I say to the reader: You need to explain this; you have to recognize that on many important aspects of life things got worse for the poor, starting precisely when we kicked into high gear in the effort to help these people.

Changing Attitude Toward the Poor

Reason: In 1965 you had been an architect of the Great Society programs of President Lyndon Johnson and had been very interested in solving the problems of the poor, particularly the black poor. As you note in the book, you were very optimistic about future years. What went haywire starting in the mid-1960s?

Murray: We had, first, a change in our attitude toward who the poor are and why they are poor or why they are ill-educated or why they commit crimes. That change consisted very simply of deciding that the system is to blame. It was logically appropriate for us to do the things we did with the Great Society programs once you granted the basic premise that the system is to blame, that it's not the fault of the people we're trying to help. Unfortunately, in the process of making those changes, we sent a terrible message to all people, but especially the young people. We said, "You don't need

99

to feel any sense of chagrin at the situation you're in. Even if you do make an effort to try to improve your situation, it's not at all clear that it's going to do any good, because the system is so locked in against you."

Reason: You say that the rules changed between 1960 and 1980 for some people, particularly the young and particularly the poor, but not for the affluent members of society. How was it that these people on the bottom of the economic totem pole got a different message?

A New Course Is Needed

A new course is surely needed. In 1959, 23 percent of poor families were headed by females. In 1982, after billions of dollars of welfare programs and the massive efforts of the War on Poverty, and after welfare expenditures in 1980 *twenty-one times* the levels of expenditures in 1950, the proportion of female-headed households in poverty had increased to 48 percent. This destruction of families is unprecedented. The Catholic tradition cannot possibly be used to defend it. What is wrong? What needs to be changed in the *design* of public policy?

Despite immense and unprecedented expenditures to eliminate poverty, the poverty level in the U.S. hit its lowest historical plateau at 11 percent in 1973, climbed back up to 13 percent in 1980, and to 15 percent in 1982. The sums of money being spent to eliminate poverty exceed by far the sums necessary to lift every man, woman and child in the U.S. above the poverty line. Something clearly absurd is going on.

Michael Novak, *Human Life Review*, Spring 1984.

Murray: Well, let's take the classic example of welfare. In the book, I take a pair of youngsters, Harold and Phyllis—they aren't necessarily black, Oriental, or Caucasian. They don't necessarily live in the slum, but they come from low-income parents and they have average ability, average education, and average skills. In 1960, if Phyllis finds herself pregnant, her only real option is to convince Harold to marry her or give the baby up for adoption. I mean there is AFDC (Aid to Families with Dependent Children), but that's a lousy life, because it's very small payment. There are no other sources of support. She can't get a job, because then she'll lose her benefits; and she can't live with Harold or else she will lose her benefits. Just from a very commonsense point of view, she has to do something about that situation and not try to bring up the baby herself. By 1970, 10 years later, the situation has changed drastically. She can get the equivalent of a minimum-wage income by putting together a package of AFDC, Medicaid, food stamps, subsidized housing, and the rest of it. She may now live with Harold without losing her benefits, which is an extremely important change. In all of these ways, what made sense in 1960 no longer necessarily makes sense. If she wants to be with Harold, one thing is quite clear: it would be disastrous for them to be married, because once they're married then she will lose many of these benefits. So the same young couple that very likely would have gotten married in 1960 won't get married in 1970. And a woman who very possibly would not have kept a child is now raising the child. They are responding to the reality of the world around them.

Dispossessing the Poor

Reason: One of the most striking aspects of your book is your very meticulous outlining of the process by which one set of poor people is dispossessed in favor of another set of poor people. How did this develop, and why is it allowed to go on?

Murray: We decided in the mid-1960s that all poor people are the same: they are all poor. We know they're poor because we have defined a poverty line, and they're all underneath it. So that's one aspect of it. The other aspect is, if it's not your fault that you are a student who is constantly assaulting the teacher, then it becomes very awkward to *credit* the student who is sitting there and studying hard. If you give that student credit, aren't you implying that the good student has something to do with his goodness, and doesn't that force you to admit the bad student has something to do with his badness?

We simply did not think about the very large population of poor people out there who are holding down jobs and trying to raise their kids right and hate crime and think people ought to obey the law and support themselves and do well in school. They just became invisible....

Reason: I'd like to give you a chance to respond to some critics of your central thesis. First of all, there's the argument that the economy in general took a tailspin starting in the mid-to late '60s, and the downward trends you note simply followed the economy at large.

Murray: The changes in the indexes of unemployment occurred not at the end of the '60s, when the economy started to go bad. They occurred in 1965-67, '68, when the economy was overheated, when the overall unemployment was under 4 percent and for males in particular was under 3 percent. So it's kind of hard to appeal to a disintegrating economy to explain those trends.

Reason: What about the idea that the workforce experienced a massive increase, that you had all these young people coming into the workforce and crowding out people for jobs? You also had an enormous increase in the 15-25 population, which caused the great bulk of crime and overload of the schools during that period and what not. What's your response to this sort of a "demographic argument"?

Murray: For the economic indicators, part of the response is the same comment I made earlier. You're talking about an economy which was showing no signs of being unable to absorb people in the '60s. And on the question of crime, the increases in crime are seen even after controlling for the changing age and other demographic statistics.

Is Federal Welfare Workable?

Reason: Still another comment on your book is that you were attacking sort of a generic welfare, when in fact it's not welfare that's bad—it's the sort of programs we have put in place under social welfare. How do you deal with that criticism?

Murray: When I got to the end of the book and was trying to put together my ideal system, I was not philosophically opposed to installing a federally run system that tried to correct these things, but I could not construct a system that I believed in myself. Any system I could concoct for myself and try to imagine what would happen if it were actually put in place ran into the problem that the downward-pulling incentives were greater than the upward-pushing ones. The 19th-century British intellectuals of whom Gertrude Himmelfarb writes so fascinatingly in her book *The Idea of Poverty* were right when they dealt with the true difficulties of trying to give something to somebody and at the same time do good for them. It's ironic that we pass off as being sort of a pop-wisdom notion that you do more harm than good by trying to help people. A little bit of intellectual history would help us a lot here....

Monstrous Bureaucratic Mess

The plethora of Welfare programs and civil-rights legislation enacted and expanded upon over the last twenty years would, we were told at the beginning, vanquish poverty in America by eliminating such problems as slums, inadequate housing, ignorance, disease, crime, and unemployment. Our "Liberal" policy makers have since given us a monstrous, sprawling, bureaucratic Welfare State whose tentacles have insinuated themselves into housing, health, education, agriculture, and virtually every other aspect of American life.

Gary Allen, *American Opinion*, December 1984.

Reason: What are your specific policy suggestions in welfare, education, and crime?

Murray: I will begin by saying that the tenor of the last part of the book is: I'm going to lay out some moral problems for you. In the very last chapter I do this in terms of proposals. The first one has to do with affirmative action. I think we ought to strip our laws and regulations of everything that rewards or recommends or requires preferential treatment by race. I think that is one of the single most unfortunate changes of the 1960s and it is one that we can change at no cost. Then I could take on two other proposals. The first is in education, and I'd say let's give vouchers or some other form of aid to parents which enables the free market to work in education. I probably have gotten more instead of less radical on this one since I wrote the book. I am increasingly ready to junk the public school system. The reason for doing this in terms of poor people is that you have lots of parents out there who, given the opportunity, would go out and interview teachers and select schools just the way middle-class parents do when they send their kids to private schools, and they would do a very good job of it and they would finally get schools that operate on the same principles they do. Some parents won't behave that way, but my response is, how have you lost?—because the schools right now are not educating our children in the inner city.

The other proposal was the most interesting and the one that's gotten the most attention. I simply say this: I have a plan that would unquestionably make steady workers out of most people who are now considered not job-ready, which would make the numbers of illegitimate children to single teenagers plunge, and would do a number of other good things—including, by the way, restoring status to that working class that most deserves it. That proposal consists of scrapping the whole thing, getting rid of everything in the whole social welfare system. Having done that, let's look around and see what the world looks like and see what we can do to even make further improvements. And I say, well, I'll put back unemployment insurance. But once I've done that, my argument is: just what kinds of people are left that need help that can't expect to get it through locally funded services? I would say that in this proposal perhaps the punchline comes at the end, where I've offered the choice to my readers that they would make if they knew their own children were going to be orphaned. Would they put their own children with a family that was so poor that their children would be ragged and some days would be hungry, but they would be sent to school and would be taught to value independence? Or would they put their children with parents who would not send them to school, would not teach them such values, but would have plenty of food and clothing given to them by others? To me the answer is obvious, and I'm trying to get readers to realize the ways in which they are making the other choice for other people's children.

Local and State Agencies

Reason: When you refer to local services, do you mean local government services or private agencies?

Murray: I'm not too specific about that in the book, because I figure I antagonize people enough already by getting rid of the federal system. My own feeling is that it is very difficult even to have good municipal services because of the inherent problems in deciding who gets help and who doesn't. I believe in the free market in lots of different ways, and one of the ways I believe in the free market is that it throws forth services that are most badly needed more or less to the extent that they are needed. It also is pretty good in calibrating how to deliver those services. I don't have much faith in governments to do that.

Reason: When you say, "Throw out the whole system," you're talking everything but unemployment insurance and Social Security?

Murray: Yes, I don't deal with the elderly in the book, so I don't deal with Social Security. Otherwise you've stated it correctly—the whole shebang, from food stamps to AFDC and the rest.

Hungry Children

Reason: What about the hungry children?

Murray: The hungry children? Well, let's talk about hungry children, if you don't like it when I say that I'd get rid of food stamps. Let's back off a minute and think about hungry children. If it is true that malnourished children in this country are predominantly youngsters who are malnourished because their parents cannot afford to give them an adequate diet, then food stamps make sense. If, however, malnourishment of children in this country is predominantly a problem of a parent who is feeding a baby on soft drinks and potato chips, to take an example that unfortunately is not drawn out of thin air—if that is the nature of the problem, then food stamps are not going to help. I submit to you as an empirical statement that the vast majority of malnourished children in this country are of the latter type. So don't talk to me about hungry children unless you are prepared to ask why they are malnourished, which is a better word than hungry, and what "generous" programs will do for them.

Furthermore, can you imagine in the absence of federal programs that a hungry child in this country is going to go on without anybody being willing to help? I'm willing to accept the responsibility that you are always going to have problems in coverage, as indeed you have problems in coverage of food stamps. But the notion that there are not going to be people ready and eager to feed hungry children is absurd and ahistorical....

What We Owe the Poor

Reason: Now we're going to finish up on a philosophical note here. What do we owe the poor?

Murray: A chance. Let me put it another way. When I am trying to decide what kind of social policy I want, I say to myself, "What would I want if I were a parent with little money trying to raise kids." I would want them to have a chance at an education. I would want there to be a job out there if I went out and looked for it hard enough. I would want to be safe in my person. I would want my children to be safe. I would want to be secure in my possessions—I guess rights of property, even though I would have very little property. After that, I really find a lot longer list of things I *wouldn't* want if I were poor. I don't want somebody coming down into my neighborhood and telling my daughter that it's okay for her to have a baby—not when I'm telling her the opposite. I don't want someone to come into the school and tell my son that it's not his fault that he's not doing well on the test. There's a whole list of things like that that I look around right now and see I *would* get if I were poor.

A Moral Element

So, what do we owe the poor? We owe them a chance, we owe them opportunities that they can make good on, with no guarantees, but most of all with no penalties for success.

Reason: Finally, you say as a general rule that compulsory transfers from one poor person to another are uncomfortably like robbery. Is there a moral element in government welfare programs?

Murray: Yes, I see a morality problem, but one on which I'm willing to compromise. It is my own personal view that the government has very limited rights in what it can do to me, including taking my property to use on behalf of others. And even if I'm in the middle class, for them to take money that I have earned and spend it on these programs is wrong. They don't have that right. On the other hand, when I say I'm willing to compromise, it is because, yes, I've paid too much taxes, but I still get along okay. So I'm not going to go to the barricades for that.

"The welfare system provides for the majority of recipients precisely what most Americans... believe it should: a temporary safety net to ease the burden of hard times."

Government Programs Aid the Poor

Richard D. Coe and Greg J. Duncan

The welfare system in the US was developed in order to, among other things, increase the standard of living for the poor, and provide them with opportunities that may not have been normally a possibility. In recent years, these programs have been continually under attack, and the welfare program has been accused of being costly and extremely inefficient. In the following viewpoint, the authors attack Mr. Murray's (the author of the previous viewpoint) conclusions as being factually and morally inadequate, believing that welfare does indeed provide help for the poor. Richard D. Coe is associate professor of economics at the New College of the University of South Florida. Greg J. Duncan is senior study director in the Survey Research Center of the University of Michigan.

As you read, consider the following questions:

1. According to the authors, how long do most welfare recipients remain on welfare? How does this contradict a long-standing myth?
2. One accusation leveled at welfare is that it is responsible for breaking up families. Do the authors believe this? Why or why not?

In his book *Losing Ground*, Charles Murray carries the neoconservative critique of Great Society social policies to its logical
extreme. He argues that the programs launched in the 1960s have
not only failed to help the disadvantaged, but have actually created
dependency by discouraging work; breaking up families, diluting
the quality of education and promoting out-of-wedlock births.
Mr. Murray thinks the U.S. would be better off eliminating all
federal welfare programs. "Cut the knot," he urges, asserting that
"the lives of large numbers of poor people would be radically
changed for the better."

This is strong stuff and calls for convincing evidence to warrant
the attention it has received. However, his argument rests primarily
on 30 years of annual Census Bureau statistics on poverty, family
instability, crime and employment. Mr. Murray himself notes that
such information, obtained from annual cross-sectional surveys,
is not well-suited for disentangling causation or even describing the
longer-term position of particular population groups. Successive
annual counts may show unchanging numbers of welfare recipients or numbers of poor people but cannot reveal whether those
numbers are made up of an unchanging group. "What we would
really like," he writes, "is a longitudinal sample of the disadvantaged."

The PSID

In fact, there is such a longitudinal study, and it provides a much
clearer view of some of the issues Mr. Murray wishes to address.
For the past 18 years, the University of Michigan's Panel Study of
Income Dynamics has been tracking the economic fortunes of a
large representative sample of U.S. families—both the disadvantaged and the advantaged. The PSID does not reach back into the
1950s, as the Census Bureau's data can, nor cover all the issues
addressed (crime, school quality) or ignored (nutrition, infant mor-
tality) by Mr. Murray, but it does provide a wealth of information
on patterns of work, on welfare use and on family composition
changes ever since the Great Society programs were begun. In 10
volumes of detailed analysis, in articles by numerous independent
researchers and in the summary book *Years of Poverty, Years of
Plenty*, the PSID reveals a picture of economic mobility and of
generally benign welfare programs that differs dramatically from
Losing Ground.

Not a Long-Term Experience

Mr. Murray's attack on the core social programs—Aid to Families
With Dependent Children and food stamps—is based on the
premise that they foster dependency by discouraging work and
marriage and reduce the stigma formerly attached to a life on the
dole. He concludes, with regret, that these programs cannot be
regarded as insurance against temporary misfortune, nor are they

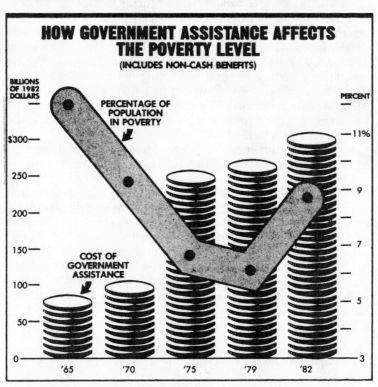

HOW GOVERNMENT ASSISTANCE AFFECTS THE POVERTY LEVEL
(INCLUDES NON-CASH BENEFITS)

BILLIONS OF 1982 DOLLARS

PERCENTAGE OF POPULATION IN POVERTY

PERCENT

$300—
250—
200—
150—
100—
50—
0—

COST OF GOVERNMENT ASSISTANCE

—11%
— 9
— 7
— 5
— 3

'65   '70   '75   '79   '82

Gail McCrory for *The Washington Post*. Reprinted with permission.

an acceptable means of providing a minimally adequate diet or home environment for needy children.

The facts, as shown by PSID data, are remarkably inconsistent with his assumptions.

Fact: Welfare use is not typically a long-term experience. The typical spell of welfare receipt is fairly short—half extend for periods of no more than two years and only one in six lasts for more than eight years. While 50 million Americans lived in families that received some welfare income during the 1970s, only five million could be characterized as persistently dependent on it.

Fact: Most welfare recipients mix work and welfare during the years in which welfare is received. Fewer than half of the people who received welfare, whether for a single year or over many years, relied on it as the source of more than half of their total family income over a given period.

Fact: Welfare dependency is not typically transmitted from one genera-tion to the next. The PSID study of the women who grew up in families that depended heavily upon welfare in the late 1960s and early 1970s found that the vast majority—four-fifths—were not themselves heavily dependent upon welfare once they left home and established independent households. For black women, there was no significant link between their welfare status and that of their parents.

Fact: Mr. Murray's assertions notwithstanding, there is no conclusive evidence of strong links between the generosity of existing welfare programs and the incidence of births, divorces, marriages or remarriages. The most comprehensive study of this issue, by Harvard researchers David Ellwood and Mary Jo Bane, completed after *Losing Ground* was written, concluded that "welfare simply does not appear to be the underlying cause of the dramatic changes in family structure of the past few decades."

In short, typical welfare spells are brief, interspersed with work, do not break up families and are not passed on from parent to child.

The temporary nature of most welfare spells is part of the much larger picture of economic mobility painted by the PSID data. Ours is clearly a dynamic society in which individual and family economic fortunes undergo substantial change. It can correctly be inferred from these longitudinal data that the longer-term distribution of income and, quite likely, economic opportunity are indeed more equal than single-year figures would indicate. This evidence is fundamentally inconsistent with Mr. Murray's view that the welfare system invariably produces persistent poverty and dependency.

A Significant Number

A look behind the general mobility shows that these changes are frequently for the better, but some are for the worse and many—favorable and unfavorable—appear to result from events largely beyond the control of the individual. Misfortunes are not limited to the lower end of the income scale; their damaging effects can touch all economic levels. Anyone familiar with the economic circumstances of divorced women and their children, who are nearly three times as likely to fall into poverty as divorced men, or with the consequences of a sudden disability or layoff can corroborate this fact. Given time, however, such setbacks are usually overcome as individuals seize some new opportunity provided by a dynamic society to rebuild their lives. In the meantime, the welfare system provides for the majority of recipients precisely what most Americans, including Charles Murray, believe it should: a temporary safety net to ease the burden of hard times.

The darker side of this picture of mobility is the plight of the individuals left behind in its wake. Even with welfare payments added to family income, more than one-tenth of all children (and nearly half of black children) spent a substantial portion of their childhood in poverty. And while they constituted a small fraction of all those who came into contact with welfare, the number of people spending most of the 1970s in welfare-dependent families was far from insignificant—totaling some five million. Since these long-term recipients tend to accumulate on the rolls, they account for a disproportionate share of total program expenditures.

Encouraging Evidence

Why do the parents in these persistently dependent families fail to work their way off welfare? Perhaps, as Charles Murray suggests, the unintended incentives of the welfare system played a role. For many, however, even year-round employment in the jobs typically available to them would fail to lift their families out of poverty. Although we are far from understanding the relative importance of discrimination, unemployment, low skills, child-care availability and welfare disincentives in this process, there is encouraging experimental evidence from the Manpower Development Research Corporation to indicate that job-skills programs offer hope for moving long-term welfare recipients into the labor force.

===

Puzzling Conclusion

The casual dismissal of the post-1965 programs as ineffective in reducing poverty is puzzling.

It is indisputable that the initiatives of the Johnson-era war on poverty, and actions taken in the Nixon administration that followed it, substantially enlarged New Deal income-support programs and added a battery of new "safety net" devices.

From the start of the Kennedy administration to the end of the Ford administration, the federal government vastly increased the flow of aid to the poor, the near-poor, the elderly, the disabled and the jobless.

Spencer Rich, *Washington Post National Weekly Edition*, May 21, 1984.

===

Where does all this leave the welfare debate? Charles Murray sees welfare as a sinister, debilitating force, creating more poverty than it alleviates. But he and other neoconservative writers have simply failed to digest the emerging facts about the dynamic nature of welfare use. We see the system as an indispensable safety net in a dynamic society, serving largely as insurance against temporary misfortune and providing some small measure of equal opportunity in the home environments of children who, after all, constitute the majority of recipients. Viewed in this light, Mr. Murray's proposal that we eliminate welfare for the good of the poor is a cruel joke at best. Despite the welfare system's flaws, its misdirected initiatives and its potentially perverse incentives, it has in fact provided economic assistance to millions of needy Americans without trapping them into dependency.

Distinguishing Bias from Reason

The subject of welfare often generates great emotional response in people. When dealing with such a highly controversial subject, many will allow their feelings to dominate their powers of reason. Thus, one of the most important critical thinking skills is the ability to distinguish between opinions based upon emotion or bias and conclusions based upon a rational consideration of the facts.

Most of the following statements are taken from the viewpoints in this chapter. The rest are taken from other sources. Consider each statement carefully. *Mark R for any statement you believe is based on reason or a rational consideration of the facts. Mark B for any statement you believe is based on bias, prejudice, or emotion. Mark I for any statement you think is impossible to judge.*

If you are doing this activity as a member of a class or group, compare your answers with those of other class or group members. Be able to explain your answers. You may discover that others will come to different conclusions than you. Listening to the reasons others present for their answers may give you valuable insights in distinguishing between bias and reason.

If you are reading this book alone, ask others if they agree with your answers. You will find this interaction very valuable.

> *R = a statement based upon reason*
> *B = a statement based upon bias*
> *I = a statement impossible to judge*

1. The depression was the worst crisis this country has ever faced.

2. If you give a beggar money, it follows he will have more than he did before.

3. Our American system at one time required that municipal, county and state governments should use their own resources and credit before seeking such assistance from the federal treasury.

4. In any crisis, self-help is always preferable to federal assistance.

5. If the one working member of a family is poor, then the family will be poor.

6. The means for rescuing the poor requires federal effort and federal funds.

7. We have, of course, no hope of erasing poverty if we listen to that new and interesting cult which call themselves the modern conservatives.

8. A study on the poor stretching over 20 years will most likely be stronger than one stretching over five years.

9. This great nation will endure through any ill, will revive and prosper.

10. The facts show in the PSID study do not coincide with Mr. Murray's findings in his book, *Losing Ground*.

11. I am confident that our people have the resources, the initiative, and the courage to solve our present crisis.

12. The help being daily given by charity is greater than what our federal treasury can afford. If we rely on those federal funds, the poor will get less than they are getting now.

13. The conservative who votes against welfare is engaged in the search for a superior moral justification for selfishness.

14. "Welfarism" poses a grave threat to our economy.

15. Welfare should be a private concern, promoted by individuals and families.

16. I base my expectations of American charitable giving on estimates of charitable giving over the past ten years.

17. Federal aid weakens the sturdiness of our national character.

Bibliography

The following bibliography deals with the subject matter of this chapter.

Howard Baetjer Jr.	"Does Welfare Diminish Poverty?" *The Freeman*, April 1984.
Michael Bernick	"How Welfare Can Work," *The Washington Monthly*, September 1985.
Teresa Funiciello	"Welfare Mothers Earn Their Way," *Christianity & Crisis*, December 10, 1984.
John Kenneth Galbraith	"How to Get the Poor Off Our Conscience," *Harper's*, November 1985.
John C. Goodman	"Welfare Is Breeding Poverty," *Conservative Digest*, January 1985.
John McKnight	"A Reconsideration of the Crisis of the Welfare State," *Social Policy*, Summer 1985.
Charles Murray	"Helping the Poor: A Few Modest Proposals," *Commentary*, May 1985.
Charles Murray	"Saving the Poor from Welfare," *Reason*, December 1984.
Newsweek	"The Homeless: Out in the Cold," December 16, 1985.
Spencer Rich	"Look Again: The Anti-Poverty Programs Do Work," *The Washington Post National Weekly Edition*, May 21, 1984.
William Ryan	*Equality*. New York: Pantheon Books, 1981.
Robert J. Samuelson	"Escaping the Poverty Trap," *Newsweek*, September 10, 1984.
James T. Schall	"War and Poverty," *Catholicism and Crisis*, May 1984.
Society	"Safety Nets and Welfare Ceilings," January/February 1986. Special issue on welfare.
Carol Twopines	"My Life in Crime," *The Progressive*, August 1985.
U.S. News & World Report	"Welfare in America: Is It a Flop?" December 24, 1984.
Mary West	"How Far Does the Line Go Back?" *America*, March 9, 1985.

Socialism Today

Introduction

In his controversial book, *The Economics of Feasible Socialism*, socialist Alec Nove writes, "Marx's economics is either *irrelevant*, or *misleading*, or both, in respect of the problems that must be faced by any socialist economy which could exist." Using a highly critical view of Karl Marx's theories, Mr. Nove forecasts a vision of the future unlike Marx's grand ideals: he expects a socialist system that is not perfect but is more fair than current capitalist and communist systems.

Like Mr. Nove, the authors in this final chapter consider past economic ideas and then predict socialism's future. Their predictions vary because of the differences in their interpretations of those ideas. For example, some of author Robert Kuttner's beliefs are derived from John Maynard Keynes, a British economist who was especially influential in the 1930s. Keynesian economics advocates a planned economy and deficit spending by government to circulate money and stimulate recovery. On the other hand, John Hospers, a prominent Libertarian philosopher, is influenced by Herbert Spencer, the advocate of social Darwinism. Social Darwinists believe those who are the strongest economically will survive and government should not help people who fail to prosper.

Another example is that of John Buell, who believes life's value has been diminished because society requires people to live in accord with the systems it has constructed, rather than in accord with nature. His ideas are influenced by the philosopher Jean Jacques Rousseau, who wrote *The Social Contract*. In contrast, George Gilder enthusiastically embraces the machine age. To him it is a thriving era for the entrepreneurs who take risks to create the wealth which improves everyone's lives.

Marx's utopian vision of socialism never fully materialized. As a result, the crucial question debated in this chapter is whether and how a socialist system can work.

"Private enterprise gives a much truer reflection of human nature than socialism...does."

Socialism Ignores Human Nature

David Smyth

In the following viewpoint, David Smyth argues that socialism cannot work because it expects humans to behave in ways contrary to their nature. He believes that socialist societies can exist only if they use force to make people act against their nature. Conversely, capitalist societies thrive because people acting in their own best interests will benefit society at large. Mr. Smyth is a journalist and free-lance author.

As you read, consider the following questions:

1. Why does the author believe force would be necessary for a socialist system to work?
2. Why do American farms produce more than Soviet farms?
3. How does Mr. Smyth believe private enterprise encourages people to produce?

David Smyth, "Until Shrimp Learn To Whistle," *The Freeman*, September 1983.

Some things are so self-evident that they really require no proof. They are simply a matter of looking around you in your daily life to see how things work and how people act.

For example, consider these questions, and answer them from your own experience and observation of life:

—A high wind has blown over all the garbage cans down a suburban street. Food wrappers, old newspapers, and assorted scraps are strewn all over the street, sidewalks and homeowners' front yards. The residents are more likely to: A) clean up the street and sidewalks only, or B) to clean up their own front yards only.

—A sewer pipe has clogged in a 10-story apartment house. The toilet and bath-water from the top nine stories is spilling out all over the floors of the apartments and public corridors of the first floor. The first-floor dwellers are more likely to get to work at once: A) cleaning up the public corridors, B) cleaning up their own apartments.

—A widget company tries an experiment. It puts half of its salesmen on a regular salary, so that they make the same amount of money weekly regardless of how many or how few widgets they sell, or indeed whether they sell any at all. The other half are told they will be paid 25 per cent of the sales price of every widget they sell. Who will sell the most widgets: A) the first group? or B) the second group?

Human Choices

These examples could be multiplied endlessly, covering every human activity in the nation, so that overall they reflect what is known as the national economy. In each case the choice is between A) acting in the interest of society as a whole, or B) acting in one's own interest.

You may note that A) and B) do not necessarily exclude each other. Once you have wiped up the dirty bath water off the floor of your own apartment you may well decide to help your neighbors clean up the corridors of their apartments. Or you may leave it to the janitor. After all, that is what he is paid for. You may decide to help only the neighbors you are friendly with, or who are crippled or aged. Or to help clean up the corridors because the janitor is away on vacation. Whatever you decide, they are *voluntary* decisions that you alone make and that nobody imposes on you.

Meeting Responsibilities

Now, from what I have seen around me in the United States I think it is a safe bet that almost everybody will clean up his front yard before he thinks of getting to the public sidewalk, that he will mop up the mess in his own apartment before he gets around to the public corridors, and that he will sell a lot more widgets if he knows that every extra one he sells means extra money to support himself and his family.

117

Selfishness? Well, yes, in part. But in large part it is rather a matter of responsibility, of priorities. If you have a family to support that is your first duty. If you have a property it is your responsibility to maintain it. It is not your obligation to be a garbage collector for the neighborhood unless you have contracted for the job.

I have lived in other countries, in South America and in Europe, and from what I saw there I think those people too would act the same way as they do in the United States.

Acting in One's Own Interest

My observations, therefore, lead me to the conclusion that it is a universal human trait to act in one's own self-interest. It is not, in my experience, a universal human trait to act spontaneously and consistently in the public interest.

Do you agree with me so far?

Withering Away

Socialism,...will wither away when we fix our attention on a better idea....

Here is the way things should be: each person with eyes on his own aspirations, spiritual and material, not on another's satisfaction. When each makes the most of himself or herself—enlightened self-interest—then each becomes your and my servant unknowingly. Paradoxical as it sounds, in a free society, with all too human exceptions, every man and woman is going about doing what he or she wants to do.

Richard H. Crum, *The Freeman*, February 1984.

If you do, then it must also be self-evident to you at this point that private enterprise gives a much truer reflection of human nature than socialism or communism or any kind of collectivism does.

Private enterprise, private ownership, private action—they all require only one basic condition: that individual human beings will consistently and spontaneously act in their own self-interest.

Use of Force

Socialism, communism, public ownership, collectivist action, all require a quite different condition: that individuals will consistently and spontaneously act in the public interest.

Since we know from our own personal experience that people all around the world are not always likely to fulfill this basic requirement of their own accord, the consequence is inevitable and obvious: they must be *forced* to act in the public interest.

If they are not so forced, then socialism, communism or any other kind of collectivism *simply will not work*. By the very nature of their most basic assumption, these isms unavoidably lead to the use of force to make people do what they would not do spontaneously of their own accord. The use of force is imbedded in their very essence. The immediate result of such a system is the imposition of rules, regulations, requirements, quotas, work-norms, rations, inspectors, regulators, policemen and enforcers of all kinds. The end result is the Nazi concentration camp, the Soviet forced labor camp, the Vietnamese re-education camp, the Chinese collective farm and the Maoist "cultural revolution," and the Pol Pot genocide in Cambodia.

Basic Fact of Human Nature

But the use of force achieves absolutely no advance toward the ideal of a happy, free and productive society that the collectivist "idealists" perhaps sincerely wish to achieve. Since it ignores the basic fact of human nature, the collectivist system merely sinks deeper and deeper into a police society where the carrot of incentive counts for less and less while the stick of authority counts for more and more. The growing use of force merely makes the forced laborers even more recalcitrant, mutinous and uncooperative than they were to begin with (as the Communist authorities happen to be discovering right now in Poland).

Given these circumstances and this attitude, it is no accident that a privately owned American farm will outproduce a Soviet or Chinese state farm fifty- or a hundred-fold. The American farmer has the powerful incentive of self-interest inducing him to produce. The American farmer also has better equipment? Yes, but that, too, is a result of the private enterprise system. And even with the very best agricultural machinery, the Soviet state farm employee has no incentive even to keep up his machines. Combines and threshers rust out in the open fields, harvested grain rots rain-sodden out in the open. As there is no profit or benefit in it for the individual state farm employee, what does he care? Only the fear of punishment by the authorities will stimulate him to the extra effort that farming invariably requires at critical times of the year.

Benefits of Private Enterprise

If you have followed me so far, we are now agreed on this:

Firstly, the private enterprise system is based on a realistic appraisal of human nature, whereas communism or socialism is based on an "idealistic" conception of what human nature *ought* to be. And when individuals like you and me do not live up to this "ideal" then the collectivist authorities have to use force on them to oblige them to conform to the "ideal" pattern.

Secondly, the private enterprise system is in its very essence a system of individual freedom, because by the very nature of things nobody has to be forced to act in his own self-interest. He does it naturally.

Thirdly, the private enterprise system is a more productive

119

system, because everybody is motivated to produce more by the knowledge that his own efforts will have a direct, measurable effect on improving his own individual situation. In the collectivist system the individual is motivated mainly by fear of punishment, since he has no great hope of any measurable reward for his own individual efforts.

Castles in the Air

Since all our reasoning above is based on observed facts, it is pure realism. It takes the world as it is and builds on that as a secure foundation. The collectivists start out with an "idea" of the world as they think it ought to be, and they try to force people to build castles in the air that soon turn out to be prisons and hells on earth.

But the collectivist "idealists" are obstinate in their error, and not even decades of experience have persuaded them that their argument is vitiated in its first premise, that it is quite literally baseless. As Soviet dictator Nikita Khrushchev put it so picturesquely: "Those who wait for the Soviet Union to abandon Communism will wait until shrimp learn to whistle."

Disproving Socialist Propaganda

While self-interest has always been at the heart of capitalism, it has also been accompanied by a feeling of human charity and a sense of social responsibility toward one's fellow man....

With the rebuilding of sound national moral foundations and the strengthening of individual character, capitalism can continue to disprove socialist propaganda by meeting the needs and fulfilling the dreams of every citizen willing to put forth efforts at self-improvement and responsible social consciousness.

Dennis L. Peterson, *The Freeman*, October 1985.

Communists pride themselves on an "objective" interpretation of history. Those of us who have an objective view of human nature, as contrasted with their "idealistic" view of it, might well set Khrushchev's words back in his teeth: if you think your collectivist system is ever going to equal the private enterprise system in truth, freedom, or prosperity, comrade, you can wait until shrimp learn to whistle.

"[In a socialist society] labor would be truly creative activity, activity in which we could affirm ourselves and our human nature."

Socialism Affirms Human Nature

Richard Whitney

The compatibility of socialism and human nature is the issue Richard Whitney addresses in the following viewpoint. While capitalists argue socialism cannot work because it would force people to act against their instincts, Mr. Whitney believes human behavior under capitalism is unnatural. Socialism would make work a creative activity and eliminate the conflict between personal interests and the social good. In so doing, it would affirm the natural human desire to be creative and fulfilled, while making life fairer for everyone. Mr. Whitney is a staff writer for *The People*, a socialist newspaper.

As you read, consider the following questions:

1. What difference does Mr. Whitney believe there would be between work in a socialist society and work in a capitalist society?
2. How does capitalism condition its workers to be lazy, according to the author?
3. In the opinion of the author, how would socialism increase productivity?

Richard Whitney, "Socialism and Human Nature," *The People*, December 25, 1982. Reprinted with permission.

With the capitalist economy declining at a quickening pace, more and more working people today are looking for alternatives to a system that simply doesn't work. Socialists maintain that the answer to the economic crises facing us is socialism—a social system in which the means of production are socially owned and democratically administered by the organized producers themselves.

After all, what economic system could better serve the interests of society than one owned and democratically controlled by society itself? What economic system could better serve the interests of the individual than a rational, collectively planned one that gives individuals equal shares of power in determining economic policy and that rewards them in full measure for the labor they contribute to society?

Yet, many people believe that while socialism may sound fine in theory, it simply can't work in practice. Socialism cannot work, they say, because it is incompatible with human nature. There are many different variations on this theme.

"Human Nature" Arguments

One such contention against socialism has been variously described as the "iron law of oligarchy," what the German philosopher Nietzsche called the "will to power," or "Social Darwinism." This is the theory that people naturally strive to be better than, and have control over, other people, and that people are naturally competitive and aggressive. Thus, no matter what kind of social system you have, some—the greediest, the strongest, the smartest, or the most powerful—will inevitably rise above and dominate the others. Hierarchy, or a pecking order, is inevitable; thus socialism can't work.

Strangely enough, another theory of why socialism is incompatible with human nature is practically the reverse. This is the theory that "people need leaders." According to this cynical theory, most people are just plain stupid and need to be led by the hand and guided. Thus, socialism wouldn't work because it would put down or suppress potential leaders, the masses of workers would be incapable of providing direction, and society wouldn't accomplish anything—it would just degenerate.

Neither of these theories posits a conception of human nature that is universally applicable or consistent with reality. We know from our own everyday experiences that there are people who are greedy, ambitious and domineering, others who are docile, resigned to their lot in life and submissive, and many who have some combination of these qualities in varying degrees.

Some people, however, advance both theories simultaneously as an argument against socialism. What this combined theory argues, in essence, is that "some people are born leaders and some are born followers" and, therefore, a society predicated upon equitably shared power, such as socialism, cannot work. But what this theory boils down to is the proposition that there are genetically-based, radically different varieties of behavior patterns within the same human species, i.e., there are different intrinsic "human natures." Already this theory appears to be on rather shaky ground.

Individualism and Laziness

Another "human nature" argument is the idea that people are highly individualistic, yet socialism, it is presumed, would try to make everyone the same. Therefore, people will never accept socialism, and it could never function with any stability.

Finally, a common "human nature" argument is the notion that people are basically lazy and that socialism would destroy the incentive to produce and the incentive for self-improvement because it would eliminate unemployment and the coercive hand of the capitalists and because it would presumably reward all kinds of social labor more or less equally. Without the threat of unemployment and the capitalists' authoritarian managerial methods, without their rewards and punishments for greater or lesser productivity, the basically lazy workers will just take it easy and goof off, productivity will drop off, no new improvements or repairs will be made, and the system will just degenerate.

The Capitalist Line

The modern capitalist line is that to envisage a world without wage labour and capital is to entertain visions of the "unnatural." We are told time and time again that we have "forgotten human nature."...

Human nature is an ideological concept designed to shield those who benefit from the *status quo* against change.

S. Coleman, *Socialist Standard*, November 1982.

Moreover, without wage differentials, no one will be willing to take the more challenging or difficult jobs. As one critic asked, "Why would anyone want to be a doctor if you could do just as well sweeping floors?"

Nature or Nurture?

Before taking up these arguments, it should be kept in mind that human beings and human behavior are not solely the product of inborn human nature, whatever that may be found to encompass. Human beings and their behavior are also the product of their social environment. Therefore, if we see similar traits in people from similar social environments, it would be unscientific to conclude that these traits stem from human nature rather than a common response to a common social environment.

Socialists contend that much of what is frequently taken to be "human nature" is in fact simply human behavior or human consciousness that results from the social environment in which we live, especially the social conditioning that we are subjected to in capitalist society.

In this regard, it is also useful to remember that those who upheld previously existing social orders also used the "human nature" argument. For example, the feudal nobility argued that their system was preordained by God and was the "natural order of things." The slave-holding plantation owners of the old South similarly defended their system with the ideology that black people were naturally inferior and that it was against their nature to be free. To paraphrase Marx, every ruling class in history has invented "eternal laws of nature and of reason" with which to justify its continued rule. The capitalist class is no exception.

Are People Lazy?

With that, let us now take up the various "human nature" arguments, beginning with the last one.

Are people basically lazy? The answer to that question is not a simple one. It's fair to say that many or most working people today would love to have more leisure time if they could get it without having to sacrifice their living standards to do so. And we also know that many workers will try to slack off or "dog it" on the job when they get the chance.

Yet this is not a universal condition. We also know of the exceptions—the "workaholics"—and of the people who go crazy when they retire because they don't get the same satisfaction out of living when they can't work. So at first glance there does not appear to be any consistency to human nature on this score.

Yet as Marx pointed out in his more philosophical writings, one important aspect of the human species is that we are conscious beings—we can think logically and creatively, and apply our power of thought to the objects in the world around us. Certainly the history of civilization attests to the fact that one aspect of human nature is that we are essentially creative beings.

The reason why some people conclude that human beings are basically lazy is the nature of work in the capitalist social context in which we live today.

Work Under Capitalism

Under capitalism, those who labor labor for someone else—the capitalists. The capitalists decide what is to be produced, how it will be produced, and under what conditions. Due to the profit motive, workers are pushed to produce as much as they can in the least amount of time; the worker is oppressed on the job.

Thus, in general, work under capitalism is not creative activity. The decisions of what and how to create are made for the workers by someone else—the capitalist. Work under capitalism is but a means for the worker to survive. As Marx described it in his

Fred Wright for the *Daily World*. Reprinted with permission.

"Economic and Philosophic Manuscripts of 1844":

"...in his work, therefore, he [the worker] does not affirm himself but denies himself, does not feel content but unhappy, does not develop freely his physical and mental energy but mortifies his body and ruins his mind. The worker therefore only feels himself outside his work, and in his work feels outside himself. He is at home when he is not working, and when he is working he is not at home. His labour is therefore not voluntary but coerced; it is *forced labour*. It is therefore not the satisfaction of a need; it is merely a *means* to satisfy needs external to it. Its alien character emerges clearly in the fact that as soon as no physical or other compulsion exists, labour is shunned like the plague." (Emphasis in original.)

Under this system of alienated wage labor, it is no wonder that we often aren't productive unless pressured or threatened with unemployment. But it must not be assumed that we would therefore need the same pressure in a socialist context in order to be productive.

The reality is that it is human nature to be both productive and "lazy": productive to the extent that we can get rewards and fulfillment out of being productive; "lazy" to the extent that we need, and get fulfillment out of, leisure time. The problem is that under capitalism we get so little fulfillment out of the former that it often appears that we only want the latter.

Work in Socialist Society

How would this situation change in a socialist society? We—all of us who labor—would collectively and democratically control every aspect of production. We would decide what goods and services we want, what additions or improvements to the productive machinery we want, and in what quantities. We would decide how to produce these products, and we would thereby control their quality. We would control the pace, techniques, and conditions of production, including workplace safety and environmental quality.

In short, labor would be truly creative activity, activity in which we could affirm ourselves and our human nature. This is not to say that all forms of routine labor would be instantly eliminated. But even in that regard, we would no longer be performing such labor under oppressive conditions, and we could apply our creative initiative to the task of reducing routine labor, freeing us more and more for free creative activity.

In this context, we would not need the coercion of unemployment and management pressure to spur productivity. Our own human nature, including our material interests and our desire for more leisure time, would give us more incentive to be productive than ever before.

This would be so because there would no longer be a conflict between the individual interest and the social interest. Individual producers would be conscious of the fact that each contribution that they can make toward improving social productivity will redound to the benefit of each and every individual. In other words, the more productive each hour of labor becomes, the less labor it will take for individuals to attain a given material standard of living.

Thus, socialist society would provide a greater incentive to produce, and to improve productivity, than any of the systems that preceded it. Individual producers would no longer be exploited, but would receive the full social value of the product of their labor. They would be co-owners of the means of production as well as co-producers. We would all be working to enrich ourselves individually and collectively, not some separate class of owners.

Great Increase in Productivity

There is factual evidence that supports the thesis that socialism would result in a great increase, rather than decrease, in productivity. Since socialism has yet to be established anywhere in the world, there is no irrefutable proof as such. But there have been instances under capitalism in which individual production facilities have been taken over and run by the workers themselves, such as in the case of the Lip Watch factory in France a few years ago. There have also been cases in which capitalist firms have themselves initiated "self-management" and other experiments in which some of the secondary production decisions regarding *how* to produce, though not what to produce, were delegated to committees of workers.

In the vast majority of these instances in which workers have attained a greater measure of control over production, productivity has risen substantially....

If productivity rises substantially when workers gain control over secondary production decisions, imagine how much more productivity would rise if workers controlled the entire production process!

"Economic growth and social justice can be reconciled; they are often mutually reinforcing."

Socialism and Economic Growth Are Compatible

Robert Kuttner

Robert Kuttner contends that egalitarian societies can maintain a healthy and growing economy. In the following viewpoint, he examines several social democratic countries and concludes that if a society decides it wants to provide a socially just lifestyle for all its citizens, it can without sacrificing economic growth. Mr. Kuttner is the *New Republic's* economics correspondent and has written *Revolt of the Haves* and *The Economic Illusion: False Choices Between Prosperity and Social Justice.*

As you read, consider the following questions:

1. What does Mr. Kuttner mean when he writes "inequality is an ideological choice, disguised as an economic imperative"?
2. What is the difference between the tax policies of Japan and the United States, according to the author?
3. Why are universal entitlements programs better than programs aimed specifically at the poor?

Robert Kuttner, "Social Equity Can Be Good Economics," *Los Angeles Times*, September 30, 1984. Reprinted with the author's permission.

The ascendance of the conservative cause is helped along by a powerful myth: Social justice is somehow harmful to economic growth....It is an economic illusion held by most conservatives, and a myth newly embraced by many neo-liberals looking for a way to salvage the Democratic Party. The idea is also ratified far too glibly by almost the entire fraternity of professional economists.

According to this myth, gains to the common welfare that result from the workings of the marketplace are good, while social progress that results from social tinkering is inefficient, unnatural and, in any case, unsustainable. A market economy admittedly generates big winners and big losers. But that, supposedly, is the price a society must pay in order to have an efficient and dynamic economy. Substantial interference with the marketplace undermines the forces of economic growth—personal incentive, thrift, savings, investment, entrepreneurship, the efficient use of labor. In short, we may desire a more equal society on political grounds, but we shall pay a heavy economic price.

Gross Economic Inequality

A political democracy is based on the idea of civic equality. In a nation with professed egalitarian values, the only thing that gives gross inequality its legitimacy is the claim that inequality is necessary economics.

But that claim is factually wrong. A survey of the postwar economic history of industrial nations reveals no simple, mechanical relationship between equality and efficiency. At worst, that relationship is indeterminate. Economic growth and social justice can be reconciled; they are often mutually reinforcing.

Comparing the taxing and spending strategies and the social contracts of different industrial nations, one can find some efficient social programs that broaden the self-reliance of the non-rich—and others that lead to sloth and dependence. One can find some labor strategies that expand national output, improve productivity and reduce inequality—and others that lead to a two-class work force and high unemployment. One can identify pension programs that increase wealth, even as they broaden its distribution. One can find tax loopholes that enrich the wealthy by steering their money into absurdly unproductive uses. One can find good social medicine and bad private medicine—and vice versa.

Income Distribution

Equality and efficiency coexist in all manner of relationships. Inequality is an ideological choice, disguised as an economic imperative.

Consider these six economic illusions.

—*America must subsidize the wealthy in order to reward "capital formation."* In reality, the nations with the highest postwar savings rates have been those with more equal distributions of income and, with the exception of Japan, with larger public sectors. In Europe, the above-average savers include Austria, West Germany, the Netherlands, France and Italy, all generous welfare states. The issue is what a nation does with its savings, not how much it rewards the already wealthy.

Shamelessly Stingy

Hardly a day goes by on which some expert doesn't remind us smugly that we really can't expect to cure social ills like poverty simply by "throwing federal dollars at them." These experts are apt to go on and explain that we're wasting billions of the taxpayers' dollars on social programs that don't do a damned bit of good. The tax Scrooges among them add the caution that this sentimental waste of good money is threatening to put us all in the poorhouse....

Over twenty million senior citizens receive [Social Security] checks on the third of every month, the average amount for a retired couple today being something over $500....It is beyond question that there are millions of senior citizens, now supported at some minimal level of dignity and security, who would otherwise be living in unbearable poverty. That is the human meaning of throwing one kind of dollar at social problems. To say that all this has no effect on income inequality and the elimination—or, better, the prevention—of poverty is simply ridiculous.

The exceptionalistic programs, such as welfare and SSI [Supplemental Security Income], it is quite true, don't even begin to eliminate poverty. The reason is plain to see: we don't throw enough dollars. To the hapless people dependent on these programs, who number over fifteen million, the majority of them children, we are shamelessly, cruelly stingy.

William Ryan, *Equality*, 1981.

—*A progressive tax system is bad for economic growth.* Wrong again. The two industrial nations with the most tax loopholes, Britain and the United States, have the slowest records of productivity growth. And the nation with the stiffest rates of effective corporate income tax is, surprisingly, Japan. Real corporate tax rates on Japanese profits are about 40%. In the United States, they are less than 15%. In fact, Japan, with a gross national product one-third the size of the United States, actually collects more corporate tax revenue. One comparative study found that nations with the most loopholes to promote capital investment had the lowest investment rates.

—*Social Security depresses private savings rates.* Europe and Japan prove the contrary. As government social-security pensions have given old people a secure retirement, private savings rates have stayed surprisingly stable. Most people want to provide for a retirement beyond the social-security minimum. Even Japan, whose underdeveloped pension system a decade ago was credited with stimulating prodigious private savings habits, now has a social-security system as generous as those in Europe. And private Japanese savings haven't fallen. In fact, the shrewd Japanese deliberately run a surplus in their social-security account, so that social security *adds* to savings.

Strong Unions

—*Trade unions must contribute to inflation.* That depends on what kind of trade unions a country has. When a labor movement is weak, defensive and concentrated in a few industries (as in the United States), unions can inflate costs in organized sectors. In such an economy, unions cease being the broad representative of the underprivileged; they become just another special-interest group.

But that does not describe all U.S. unions, and it is a far cry from the only model of trade unionism. Statistically, countries with the highest rate of unionization include those with the best inflation-unemployment trade-offs. Sweden and Austria, with Europe's highest unionization rates, have enjoyed very low unemployment and below-average inflation. The reason is that when unions represent most working and middle-class people, they use their substantial influence for classwide gains—full employment, Social Security, lifetime learning and retraining opportunities and greater influence in the workplace. Such gains contribute to morale and productivity. A different kind of social contract between labor and business serves to improve both equality and efficiency.

Welfare Programs

—*Welfare programs are inherently inefficient.* Statistically, the economic laggards include countries with generous welfare systems and some with stingy ones. Britain and West Germany have public sectors of about the same size, but radically different records of economic performance. The top nations in productivity growth were entrepreneurial Japan (a nation with a rather small public sector but a great deal of public planning) and Austria, led by Social Democrats.

Many Americans now assume, with President Reagan, that social outlays should be limited to the truly needy. But anyone who has examined different social programs realizes the truth of the axiom that "programs limited to the poor make poor programs." Universal entitlement programs create a sense of community. Most of U.S. welfare for the poor is not only means-tested, but mean-spirited. The United States has a two-class welfare state, in which there is a striking difference between a local Social Security office (universal) and a local welfare office (for the certified poor) or between an inner-city emergency room (poor) or a clinic supported by Medicare (universal).

—*Supply-side economics stimulated a recovery.* It didn't. Capital

131

spending dropped steadily in 1982 and most of 1983, *after* the great supply-side tax cut was enacted. Major investing began only when a consumer spending boom, fueled by the huge deficits, made it worthwhile to invest. President Reagan, meet Lord Keynes. But the Reagan brand of Keynesian economics is built on military spending and tax cuts for the well-to-do. However, deficits that give tax relief to working and middle-class people and spend public dollars on useful civilian products work just as well.

In sum, the equality-efficiency debate is about political power, not about economic necessity. Societies that hold egalitarian values manage to find ways to have healthy economies without sacrificing equity. Societies where the wealthy hold disproportionate influence overlook positive-sum social bargains, for their leaders have a material and ideological stake in perpetuating privilege.

Working Hard

Supply-side economics holds that the rich in the United States have not been working because they have too little income. So, by taking money from the poor and giving it to the rich, we increase effort and stimulate the economy. Can we really believe that any considerable number of the poor prefer welfare income to a good job? Or that business people—corporate executives, the key figures in our time—are idling away their hours because of the insufficiency of their pay? This is a scandalous charge against the American businessperson—notably a hard worker.

John Kenneth Galbraith, *The Humanist*, September/October 1985.

Equity economics can be sound economics; the problem is maintaining a constituency for it. Today, U.S. politics is highly ideological. But class solidarity is entirely one-sided—conservatives are the ones with a clear ideological vision (social Darwinism) and a coherent theory of how the economy works.

Throughout history, the haves could be counted on for ingenious theories to justify the proposition that what served them also served the common good. That is not distressing; it is normal. It is only distressing that the claim finds such a wide audience.

"Once the enormous ball-and-chain of high taxation...was removed from every wage earner,...there would be such a resurgence of prosperity that government welfare would be quite unnecessary."

Socialism and Economic Growth Are Incompatible

John Hospers

Socialist economies can provide social justice only at the cost of economic growth, conservatives believe, whereas unfettered capitalism provides both growth and justice for its members. John Hospers, the author of the following viewpoint, argues that taking restrictions off businesses and cutting taxes would lead to greater economic growth and give everyone more money, thus making government efforts to promote social justice unnecessary. Mr. Hospers is a philosophy professor at the University of Southern California. He ran for the US presidency in 1972 for the Libertarian party, a third-party which advocates radically slashing the powers of government.

As you read, consider the following questions:

1. What distinction does the author see between justice and social justice?
2. Why does Mr. Hospers believe a voluntary, private system of welfare would be better than governments' welfare programs?

John Hospers, "Justice versus 'Social Justice,'" *The Freeman*, January 1985.

It has often been alleged that the free-market system is unjust. Criticisms of the free market constitute a very high percentage of the content of most college courses in ethics and social philosophy. It may be granted at once that no system is entirely just in every detail; there will always be cases of injustice. But the market system is by far the least unjust of all economic systems....

Individual Justice

Those who are engaged in "social engineering" often characterize the concept of individual justice...as outdated. What we need, they say, is *social* justice.

But what exactly does this term mean? If justice is treatment in accord with desert, and deserts are unequal, then justice demands that treatments also be unequal. If everyone were given the same wage regardless of effort or achievement, we would have a society in which hardly anyone would choose to work at all; in the end there would be nothing left to distribute, and starvation would stalk the land. The ideal of justice as complete egalitarianism—everyone receives the same regardless of who does what or how much, or even if they do nothing at all—is contradicted by the most elementary facts of reality. It is not the idea of forcible redistribution that deters egalitarians—they have no objections at all to that—but only the fact that once the goose has been killed it can lay no more eggs.

"Social Justice"

Proponents of "social justice" do not, then, usually demand that every person (or every family) receive the same income. For reasons of sheer survival, this is not done even in the Soviet Union. What the proponents of "social justice" do demand, however, is that everyone, regardless of effort, ability, or achievement, receive a "decent standard of living"—which in urban America may include not only food, clothing, and shelter, but a telephone, a television set, and convenient means of transportation as "necessities of life." And who shall be required to pay for these things? Those whose income is higher; "justice demands" that those who are "more fortunate" be required to contribute to those who are "less fortunate." These are the popular name tags, and the underlying assumption is that if one person has more and another less, this is solely a matter of "luck" or "fortune," as if somehow individual ability and initiative had nothing to do with improving one's lot.

It is far from clear, however, how A being forced to give part of his paycheck to B is an example of justice: it would seem to be a case of injustice to A, and a windfall for B. And even if such transfer payments should be made, should they be done in the name of justice? The basis of justice is desert; the basis of charity is need: in charity, we give to others because they need it; in justice, we receive compensation (or punishment) because we deserve it. The difference between justice and charity should not be obscured.

134

The poor are usually classified as "unfortunate" or "under-privileged," as if those who earned more had purposely deprived them. But this label, which social planners automatically attach to everyone who is below a certain level of income, applies only to some of them, certainly not to all. We must first investigate, which social planners almost never do, *why* they are poor.

1. Suppose a neighbor of yours is about to make an investment which you know to be fraudulent: he will lose everything if he makes the investment. Undeterred by your pleas, he does it anyway, and the result is that he loses everything. Would most people, including champions of "social justice," be willing to hand over part of their paychecks in perpetuity to a person who has merely been foolish?

2. Suppose a lady has been thrifty all her life, saved for her old age, and has a small house and yard; a second lady, with considerably more income, spent it all on riotous living and is now destitute. Should the first lady be required to give over part of her limited income each month to the second? (That is the way things work out under the current welfare system; but is this justice?)

Price of Government

An excessive price of government—an exorbitant tax rate—will similarly lower total revenues and the tax base, and induce a proliferation of substitutes for taxable activity: "paper entrepreneurialism," tax shelters, overseas tax havens, emigration to low-tax areas, movement to the underground or irregular economies, leisure activities, collectibles, and real estate manipulation. In an economy where the rich withdraw from productive investment several consequences follow: Opportunity declines, the gap between the rich and poor widens, social services decay, and "social justice" becomes a cry of envy rather than an economic reality.

George Gilder, *The Public Interest*, Summer 1982.

---

3. Assume that a worker has been able to pay into old-age insurance but simply failed to do so, spending everything she earned. Now she is destitute. Should others, who *have* provided in advance for their old age, be forced to hand over a portion of their savings to the person who has not so provided? To do so may be charitable, but is it just?

4. Now let us take a different kind of case. A person is ill or has a physical handicap which does not enable her to work; she would like to, but she can't and her family has no resources. Shouldn't "society" take care of her?

This is certainly the best case for welfare; but the question remains whether it should be government welfare (compulsorily paid by all wage earners) or privately financed welfare (voluntarily contributed by those who are able). Though the matter would require a lengthy discussion that is not possible here, I suggest that the persons who answer to this description are a comparatively small minority of the population, and that, once the enormous ball-and-chain of high taxation (including social security payments) was removed from every wage earner, and would-be entrepreneurs could start small businesses and take on employees without the present high probability that their enterprises will be bankrupted by taxes and regulation, there would be such a resurgence of prosperity that government welfare would be quite unnecessary: private funding would be quite adequate to the task, as it was during the first century of American history when the standards of living were much lower than they are now.

Preventing Suffering

Herbert Spencer was much wiser than today's planners when in 1884 he criticized "the tacit assumption that Government should step in whenever anything is not going right. 'Surely you would not have this misery continue!' exclaims someone, if you hint at demurrer to much that is now being said and done. Observe what is implied by this exclamation. It takes for granted, first, that all suffering ought to be prevented, which is not true; much of the suffering is curative, and the prevention of it is prevention of a remedy. In the second place, it takes for granted that every evil can be removed: the truth being that, with the existing defects of human nature, many evils can only be thrust out of one place or form into another place or form—often being increased by the change.

"The exclamation also implies the unhesitating belief...that evils of all kinds should be dealt with by the State. There does not occur the inquiry whether there are at work other agencies capable of dealing with evils, and whether the evils in question may not be among those which are best dealt with by these other agencies. And obviously, the more numerous governmental interventions become, the more confirmed does this habit of thought grow, and the more loud and perpetual the demands for intervention."

Getting Rid of Poverty

With an unfettered economy, and a minimum of charity (and most Americans have more than a minimum), the problem of poverty would become almost obsolete. Economist Thomas Sowell may have overstated the case, but he had a valid point when, in answering the question "How to get rid of poverty?" he answered, "Hold a meeting of all the leading experts on poverty somewhere in the middle of the Pacific and not let them go home for ten years. When they came back, they would discover there was no more poverty."

It will be apparent by now that the demands of "social justice" are incompatible with those of individual justice; to the extent that the first demand is met, the second must be sacrificed. If the government takes money out of Peter's wallet to put it in Paul's, it may have achieved greater equality, but not greater justice. It is impossible for individuals to receive a just wage on a free market and then be forced to part with a portion of it, for then they receive *less* than a just wage.

Business and Social Needs

Only if business, and especially American business, learns that to do well it has to do good, can we hope to tackle the major social challenges facing developed societies today. Government...cannot tackle these challenges. They can be solved only if seen and treated as opportunities. And the economic realities ahead are such that social needs can be financed increasingly only if their solution generates capital—that is, generates a profit. This, governments cannot do. But it is precisely what business is being paid for.

Peter F. Drucker, *Reason*, November 1985.

The final irony is that the ideals of the champions of "social justice" are not even achieved when they are put fully into practice. Because people will not—and cannot—produce indefinitely without compensation, the final result of massive transfer payments is equality of zero—universal destitution. That, after all, is how the excesses of the late Roman welfare state gave way to the destitution of the Dark Ages. It has happened many times in history, and it could happen again if the proponents of "social justice"—that is, enforced collectivism—push their demands so far as to cancel out the requirements of individual justice.

"We must break with growth....[and] construct a positive alternative...that places at the forefront the common needs of society's citizens."

Socialist Values Are More Important Than Economic Growth

John Buell

The following viewpoint questions a fundamental belief of economists and policy makers—the belief in the need for promoting economic growth. John Buell, the author, argues that the pursuit of higher and higher levels of economic growth has compromised social values, destroyed many community traditions, and made work meaningless. He recommends refashioning the social contract so that society's goal meets the needs of all citizens, rather than placing people in a destructive, competitive race for individual wealth. Mr. Buell is an associate editor of *The Progressive*, a liberal publication.

As you read, consider the following questions:

1. What does Mr. Buell mean by the "social contract"?
2. What does the author admire about nineteenth-century immigrant laborers?
3. What would be the advantages of breaking with economic growth, according to Mr. Buell?

John Buell, "The Poverty of Growth," *The Progressive*, July 1984. Reprinted by permission from *The Progressive*, 409 East Main Street, Madison, Wisconsin, 53703. Copyright © 1984, The Progressive, Inc.

In recent decades, American conservatives and liberals alike have based their politics on the economic assumption that steady growth is not only possible but indispensable. This premise is critically flawed, and the politics that flow from it are misguided and ultimately dangerous.

Conservatives believe that social stability is ensured by a constantly expanding gross national product which, they say, allows higher and higher levels of personal affluence. By and large, liberals share this vision, though they also look to economic productivity as the source of funding for those Government programs designed to ease the plight of the disadvantaged. And liberals sometimes contend that economic growth serves to stave off "the communist challenge," as John F. Kennedy put it in 1960.

Supply-Siders and Neoliberals

Today, economists of both persuasions see renewed growth as part of the remedy for almost every economic and social problem—from reducing the national debt to funding Social Security.

Supply-siders, whose views were prominent in the early years of the Reagan Administration, urge Americans to accept reductions in social spending so that tax rates can be eased and the savings redirected toward new plants and equipment. Such expansion, in turn, will theoretically generate needed revenues while diminishing the demand for Federal assistance programs.

Neoliberals who criticized the supply-siders' faith in "the magic of the market" likewise consider economic growth as essential. They, too, ask American workers to forego satisfaction of their immediate demands in the interest of long-term growth. Unlike conservatives, the liberals are willing to let the Government play an active role in redirecting investment to "sunset" or "sunrise" industries, but they insist that such intervention should be accompanied—and at least partially financed—by cutbacks in workers' traditional benefits.

These sundry approaches share a faith in the inevitability and indispensability of economic growth, as well as a conviction that the achievement of long-term growth requires short-term sacrifice. Conventional conservatives, neoliberals, and supply-siders all believe that American politics is paralyzed by a lack of commitment to the goal of growth and an unwillingness to pay the price.

The Social Contract

Their analysis has led to insistent calls for a new "social contract." The nature of that pact may be the most important political issue confronting us.

The existing social contract contains an inherent contradiction: By sanctioning the pursuit of private affluence, it diminishes the prospects of generating public wealth and assuring the common well-being. At the same time, it chips away at those shared values and traditions that undergird the very notion of society and community.

Unless the social contract is fundamentally refashioned around the idea of a common purpose, it will dissolve in a new wave of political authoritarianism. But today, free-market conservatives, neoliberals, and even social democrats avoid the larger question of the social contract, preferring instead to adhere to the notion that economic growth is the glue that holds our society together. They argue that renewed growth can generate the social consensus needed to lift America out of its economic and political doldrums; in this way, they subsume all discussion of the public good.

Rituals and Traditions

Many other cultures, however, reject the assumption that personal consumption and private acquisitiveness are the cornerstones of community. The ancient Greeks as well as the Christian philosophers believed instead in the rituals and traditions of the city, state, nation, or parish; this public culture, shared by all, was paramount in the *polis* and the Church.

Shared Identity

The value of, and need for, the experience of community is not just an abstract doctrine of religious teaching or ethical thought. It is deeply embedded in the human heart. Even the most rudimentary forms of human society are impossible without some sense of shared identity and communal responsibility. But almost everything about the organization of economic life in the United States is destructive of such human solidarity....

The need for community and interdependence can be a powerful force for countering an economic direction that places corporate profit before people, families, and neighborhoods and fosters growing inequality.

Danny Collum, *Sojourners*, November 1985.

The importance of ritual and tradition stems from the fact that they are shared, that everyone knows them to be shared, and that everyone participates in passing them down and reformulating them. Even today, watered-down forms of communal activity can be found in enclaves of our mass society—in the ethnic banquets, neighborhood taverns, and local congregations that call people together.

The emphasis on communal rather than individual activity inverts the standard contemporary arrangement. Instead of viewing social life as the happy byproduct of economic activity, this orientation defines social life as the primary goal, and economic activity as only one among many functions of the community.

Certain precapitalist groups manifested this communal orientation. As E.P. Thompson and Herbert Gutman have noted, immigrant laborers generally came to this country not as isolated individuals but as members of ethnic communities, sharing certain preindustrial work routines and social rituals. They did not oppose economic activity, but they kept it within the rhythms and norms of their cultural life. They shared a sense of appropriate work pace, work rules, and worker solidarity in times of unfair competition or economic distress.

But more than just common work habits sustained them, as Gutman explains: "A model subculture included friendly and benevolent societies as well as friendly local politicians, community-wide holiday celebrations, an occasional library (the Baltimore Journeyman Bricklayer's Union taxed members one dollar a year in the 1890s to sustain a library that included the collected works of William Shakespeare and Sir Walter Scott's Waverly novels), participant sports, churches sometimes headed by a sympathetic clergy, saloons, beer gardens, and concert halls or music halls and, depending upon circumstances, trade unionists, labor reformers, and radicals."

Modern Capital's Quest

The immigrants of the Nineteenth Century surrounded work with a whole way of life through which they expressed commitments to community and tradition. We need not romanticize life in that era to recognize that it contained elements of a genuinely shared common good.

Industrial capitalists attempted to shatter those commitments, which stood in the way of labor mobility and the quest for private affluence. Indeed, a large part of the program of modern capital in the Twentieth Century has been to divide workers against each other. Elaborate job ladders, pay scales, titles, and perquisites are designed so that workers will define their identities around those goods or possessions which make them different from (or better than) their fellow workers.

The process of cutting community ties has never been completed, and in some respects capitalism has benefited from these preindustrial common values. Without a commitment to neighborhood and community, it is doubtful whether any society would be viable—unless it relied on totalitarian forms of coercion.

Economic and political activity presumes that the worker and the citizen share—either tacitly or openly—a certain set of beliefs about the existence and desirability of the community and the rules that govern it. If the worker and the citizen reject them, any semblance of voluntary participation would disintegrate. Workers would withdraw their labor; citizens would withdraw their voice. And the delegitimated society would function only under the whip.

Economic growth in the Twentieth Century has provided satisfaction to many workers, but it has also strained those common visions that hold our society together and define our identity. And it is questionable whether, even during periods of affluence, monetary reward has been as widely and fully accepted a norm as sometimes assumed.

Stanley Aronowitz, writing ten years ago [1974] in *False Promises*, detected this discrepancy at the giant General Motors plant in Lordstown, Ohio. "Older workers in the plant as well as a minority of the youth admit that they have never seen this kind of money in their lives," noted Aronowitz. "But the young people are seeking more from their labor than high wages, pensions, and job security. At Lordstown, they are looking for 'a chance to use my brains' and a job 'where my high school education counts for something.'"

Dependent on Private Possessions

But opposition to the pursuit of private affluence is muted. The consumer society makes all of us dependent on private possessions: We need cars to commute to work, refrigerators to store food, television to relax. Luxuries turn into necessities, and so-called advances in our standard of living increase the demands on us. As more and more people need and own autos, the car provides less convenience and fewer satisfactions—even as life without it becomes increasingly difficult. It has been estimated that the average speed of an automobile in New York City today is less than that of the horse-drawn carriage a century ago.

Jungle Society

Our daily experiences of life under capitalism tell us that this competitive, jungle society does not and cannot work in the material interest of the majority of the population, who produce the wealth but do not possess it. Socialism becomes a meaningful idea to workers when it is realised that instead of trying to survive in conflict with everyone else, as if this were the only possible way, the answer is to survive by co-operating with the rest of humanity.

S. Coleman, *Socialist Standard*, November 1982.

In the midst of economic crisis, there remain signs that workers reject economic growth as the be-all and end-all of life. To some, the sacrifice is not worth the candle; to others, the promise of material reward rings hollow. A higher proportion of Americans reported they were "happy" in 1957 than at any time in the ensuing twenty years, even though considerable material progress was achieved during this period, notes Paul Wachtel in *Poverty of Affluence*.

Many Americans are now striving—however haltingly—to fashion alternatives to a culture of individual wealth. The growth of food cooperatives, barter arrangements, farmers' markets, and free labor exchanges over the past twenty years is but one sign that people sense the unfairness of the present industrial order. They yearn for simpler patterns of economic interaction and economic survival; they yearn for a mode of production they can understand and control.

Even cultist groups, religious fundamentalists, and right-to-lifers are symptomatic of popular resistance to a system that subordinates communal values to the quest for private gain. Most participants in such movements do not harbor a theory of resistance to economic growth, nor do they share a commitment to an *alternative* sense of the common good. In fact, the principal institutions of our society make it difficult to define alternative values.

Labor unions, especially in the American context where no sustained anticapitalist movements have ever taken hold, usually define their task as achievement of greater affluence for the worker within the capitalist structure. As a consequence, they have promoted the notion of growth as enthusiastically as the corporate managers.

The failure of the trade union leadership to offer a different course has squeezed rank-and-file resistance into inchoate, often furtive forms of protest: wildcat strikes, slowdowns, and absenteeism. Where the work force is atomized, the working class fragmented, and housing dispersed, it becomes more difficult for workers to formulate a coherent language of protest.

Break with Growth

We must break with growth, clearly and unequivocally. No half-step will suffice. We need to construct a positive alternative for our economy, one that places at the forefront the common needs of society's citizens, not the private desires of the economy's participants.

Such a restructured economy would shift the patterns of consumption toward what French socialist Andre Gorz has called inclusive, or public, goods. It would foster mass transit, communal housing, public recreation, and preventive health care. It would establish public jobs and offer low-interest loans for insulation, solar retrofitting, and other energy-efficient purposes. And it would afford local communities the opportunity to fashion their own economic goals for their own specific needs.

A society that planned the production of inclusive goods could eliminate the mountains of waste generated by the consumer system. The U.S. economy spends $100 billion a year on advertising and sales promotion; these expenditures surely could be put to more productive use. Over the years, style and model changes have accounted for roughly one-fourth the cost of each automobile; the

143

engineering and creative skills engaged in such tinkering surely could be more usefully deployed.

But the idea of a regulated economy connotes tedium and regimentation. It is the great cultural task of progressives to show that an economy that includes social planning and the production of public goods need not enslave or stultify. This is not an insurmountable task.

A Refashioned Economy

The whole point of breaking with an economy of forced growth is to allow opportunities for self-chosen, creative activity. We work too hard and too long at jobs that provide too little, if any, social value. A refashioned economy would not only produce essential public goods and services; it would free time for individuals to do as they please. And it could produce what Ivan Illich calls convivial tools: such products and technologies as modern power tools or video equipment that individuals and small groups could master and employ for themselves.

Talk of transforming the nature of production and consumption is routinely ridiculed as utopian. But failing to dream, and failing to promote the dream, consigns us all to the stagnant economics and parched politics of the present.

"All of us are dependent for our livelihood and progress...on the creativity and courage of the particular men who accept the risks which generate our riches."

Socialist Values Are Naive and Impractical

George Gilder

Socialist schemes for redistributing wealth fail to realize the role free market entrepreneurs play in creating wealth, according to George Gilder. He is a controversial and well-known author and writes regularly for several conservative magazines. His books include *Wealth and Poverty* and *Sexual Suicide*. In the following viewpoint excerpted from his book, *The Spirit of Enterprise*, Mr. Gilder argues that economic growth is necessary for human life to improve and society to be stable. Socialists who advocate distributing wealth equally, he believes, ignore the fact that it is the especially prosperous few who make everyone's life better by creating more wealth.

As you read, consider the following questions:

1. Why is economic growth necessary, according to Mr. Gilder?
2. Why does the author believe leftist economic dreams are unrealistic?
3. What does Mr. Gilder think the key to economic growth is?

The prevailing theory of capitalism suffers from one central and disabling flaw: a profound distrust and incomprehension of capitalists. With its circular flows of purchasing power, its invisible-handed markets, its intricate interplays of goods and moneys, all modern economics, in fact, resembles a vast mathematical drama, on an elaborate stage of theory, without a protagonist to animate the play....

The left fantasizes a tiny elite of tycoons wielding the powers of enterprise rather than an immense class of entrepreneurs and aspiring businessmen—perhaps 30 million in the United States alone—who comprise a near majority of working citizens....The left sees the power of business as evil and selfish in spirit and purpose....

The capitalist is not merely a dependent of capital, labor, and land; he defines and creates capital, lends value to land, and offers his own labor while giving effect to the otherwise amorphous labor of others. He is not chiefly a tool of markets but a maker of markets; not a scout of opportunities but a developer of opportunity; not an optimizer of resources but an inventor of them; not a respondent to existing demands but an innovator who evokes demand; not chiefly a user of technology but a producer of it....

Less Selfish

In their most inventive and beneficial role, capitalists seek monopoly: the unique product, the startling new fashion, the marketing breakthrough, the novel design. These ventures disrupt existing equilibria rather than restore a natural balance that outside forces have thrown awry. Because they can change the technical frontiers and reshape public desires, entrepreneurs may be even less limited by tastes and technologies than artists and writers, who are widely seen as supremely free. And because entrepreneurs must necessarily work and share credit with others and produce for them, they tend to be less selfish than other creative people, who often exalt happiness and self-expression as their highest goals.

The virtual absence of these vital and creative, tenacious and sacrificial men from the economic and moral ledgers of society depletes and demoralizes the culture of capitalism. It leads to a failure to pass on to many youths a notion of the sources of their affluence and the possibilities of their lives. It leads to a persistent illusion on the part of intellectuals that we live in an age without heroes. It leads to a widespread sense of entitlement to the bounties of "society," to a "social surplus," which in fact is the product of the labor and ingenuity of particular men and women. Society is always in deep debt to the entrepreneurs who sustain it and rarely consume by themselves more than the smallest share of what they give society....Many children of the West assume that they are entitled: that the comforts of life are natural and inevitable while its hardships are an effect of the malignity of leaders, that goods are summoned by invisible hands or disembodied social dialectics or exogenous sciences rather than contrived by the specific exertions and sacrifices of men and women on the frontiers of enterprise....

Entitled Children

While the entitled children speak of an absence of worthwhile work, the entrepreneurs hold three jobs at one time. While the entitled children ache at the burden of laboring nine to five, the entrepreneurs rise before dawn and work happily from five to nine. While the entitled children complain that success comes from "contacts" with the high and mighty—and talk of the frustrations of "politics"—the entrepreneurs ignore politics and make their contacts with workers and customers. While the entitled children see failure as catastrophe—a reason to resign—the entrepreneur takes it in stride as a spur to new struggle.

While the entitled children think riches come to the gambler or the Scrooge, to the ones blessed with genius or good connections, who exploit labor or political links, who are gifted with talent or land, natural resources or unnatural luck, entrepreneurs know that genius is sweat and toil and sacrifice and that natural resources gain value only by the ingenuity and labor of man....

Miraculous Expansion

As an antidote to some of our most serious problems, rapid U.S. growth cannot be overrated. The [recent] expansion has created nearly 7 million jobs since it began—a performance viewed by our allies...as nothing short of miraculous....

We know that only solid, sustained expansion in the economy will solve our most fundamental economic problems.

J. Richard Zecher, *The Chase Economic Observer*, July/August 1984.

It is they who chiefly create the wealth over which the politicians posture and struggle. When the capitalists are thwarted, deflected, or dispossessed, the generals and politicians, the guerrilla chieftains and socialist intellectuals, are always amazed at how quickly the great physical means of production—the contested tokens of wealth and resources of nature—dissolve into so much scrap, ruined concrete, snarled wire, and wilderness. The so-called means of production are impotent to generate wealth and progress without the creative men of production, the entrepreneurs....

Behind Leftist Prose

The essential problem of enterprise in the West is not so much the lingering appeal of socialism as an even more tantalizing vision in the minds of the political elite. Glimmering on the horizons of every social democratic platform, every neoliberal testament, every new mandate for reindustrialization, every learned demand for cooperation among business, labor, and government and an end to the adversarial spirit in American enterprise, every new citation of industrial strategy among the Japanese, every encouraging reference to the *dirigisme* of the French, every new disguise for the discredited ghost of the Reconstruction Finance Corporation from New Deal-depressed America, every call for a "fair distribution" of the burdens of change, an "equitable" reform of taxation, or a "reasonable" return on capital, every evangelical writ on the limits of growth, the scarcity of resources, the burden of population, the gap between the rich and the poor, every appeal for economic democracy, social control of corporations, and an end to untrammeled commercialism—suffusing all the most visionary and idealistic prose of leftist economics is the same essential dream of the same static and technocratic destiny: capitalism without capitalists. Wealth without the rich, choice without too many things to choose, political and intellectual freedom without a vulgarian welter of individual money and goods, a social revolution every week or so without all this disruptive enterprise....

Euthanasia of the Entrepreneur

The dream, in its always unexpected and unwanted way, is drearily coming to pass throughout the social democratic domains of Western Europe. But even in the United States the pressure mounts to move this way. The agenda is simple: the stealthy and unannounced euthanasia of the entrepreneur. It can be accomplished easily by following two seductive themes of policy: lowering tax and interest costs for large corporations and a few other favored institutions, while shifting the burden increasingly to individuals and families. By reducing corporate taxes, subsidizing corporate loans, sponsoring a wide range of favored borrowers, institutionalizing personal savings, and discreetly allowing taxes to rise on personal income, government can painlessly extinguish the disposable wealth of entrepreneurs. It can enact a bold and comprehensive program—full of stimuli for "capital formation" and "job creation," replete with policies to favor business and rhetoric to inspire Republicans—that swiftly steals in and stifles the nation's spirit of enterprise....

Need for Wealth

What the creators of the system of capitalism without capitalists fail to comprehend is that you can't have capital gains without capital, and you can't benefit from corporate subsidies without being a corporation. To start a business requires disposable personal income, and that is what high personal rates wring out of the system. British managers and executives receive pitifully low nominal incomes (why ask for more!); but they get an amazing

148

"I often think it would be nice to get the opportunity to betray my socialist principles."

array of relatively untaxable perks, from company cars to business suits, from vacation resorts to scholarships, from housing to entertainment. These benefits, which cannot be saved and invested in a new company, tie down British businessmen to the existing corporate structure: the very business establishment, cobwebbed with subtle strands of governmental dependency, that is a key obstacle to progress....

The reason the system of capitalism without capitalists is failing throughout most of Europe is that it misconceives the essential nature of growth. Poring over huge aggregations of economic data, economists see the rise to wealth as a slow upward climb achieved through the marginal productivity gains of millions of workers, through the slow accumulation of plant and machinery, and through the continued improvement of "human capital" by advances in education, training, and health. But, in fact, all these sources of growth are dwarfed by the role of entrepreneurs launching new companies based on new concepts or technologies. These gains generate the wealth that finances the welfare state, that makes possible the long-term investments in human capital that are often seen as the primary source of growth.

Encouraging Entrepreneurs

The key to growth is quite simple: creative men with money. The cause of stagnation is similarly clear: depriving creative individuals of financial power. To revive the slumping nations of social democracy, the prime need is to reverse the policies of entrepreneurial euthanasia. Individuals must be allowed to accumulate disposable savings and wield them in the economies of the West. The crux is individual, not corporate or collective, wealth. No discipline of the money supply or reduction in government spending, however heroic, no support scheme for innovation and enterprise, no program for creating jobs, no subsidy for productive investment, however generous and ingenious, can have any significant effect without an increase in the numbers and savings of entrepreneurs....

An economy is governed by the will and imagination, creativity and persistence of its entrepreneurs. All that matters is that they be encouraged, by religion and culture, law and policy, to do their work well....

All of us are dependent for our livelihood and progress not on a vast and predictable machine, but on the creativity and courage of the particular men who accept the risks which generate our riches. The machine age is the paramount era not of depersonalized masses but of individual achievement on the curve of growth.

150

Recognizing Statements That Are Provable

From various sources of information we are constantly confronted with statements and generalizations about social and moral problems. In order to think clearly about these problems, it is useful to be able to make a basic distinction between statements for which evidence can be found and other statements which cannot be verified or proved because evidence is not available or the issue is too controversial.

Readers should constantly be aware that magazines, newspapers and other sources often contain statements of a controversial or questionable nature. The following activity is designed to allow experimentation with statements that are provable and those that are not.

Most of the following statements are taken from the viewpoints in this chapter. Consider each statement carefully. *Mark P for any statement you believe is provable. Mark U for any statement you feel is unprovable because of lack of evidence. Mark C for statements you think are too controversial to be proved to everyone's satisfaction.*

If you are doing this activity as a member of a class or group, compare your answers with those of other class or group members. Be able to defend your answers. You may discover that others will come to different conclusions than you. Listening to the reasons others present for their answers may give you valuable insights in recognizing statements that are provable.

If you are reading this book alone, ask others if they agree with your answers. You too will find this interaction very valuable.

P = provable
U = unprovable
C = too controversial

1. It is a universal human trait to act in one's own self-interest.

2. A privately-owned American farm will outproduce a Soviet or Chinese state farm fifty- or a hundred-fold.

3. More and more working people today are looking for alternatives to the capitalist system.

4. US welfare programs for the poor are mean-spirited.

5. Eliminating high taxes would lead to such economic prosperity that government welfare would be unnecessary.

6. Entrepreneurs tend to be less selfish than other creative people, who often exalt happiness and self-expression as their highest goals.

7. Private enterprise gives a much truer reflection of human nature than socialism does.

8. The slave-holding plantation owners of the old South defended their system with the argument that black people were naturally inferior and that it was against their nature to be free.

9. Every ruling class in history has invented "eternal laws of nature and of reason" to justify its continued rule.

10. People are naturally aggressive and strive to be better than other people.

11. One can find some efficient social programs that broaden the self-reliance of the poor—and others that lead to sloth and dependence.

12. Socialist societies must use force to make people act in the public interest.

13. Much of what is frequently taken to be "human nature" is simply human behavior that results from the social environment in which we live.

14. Criticisms of the free market are found in a very high percentage of the content of most college courses in ethics and social philosophy.

15. All of us are dependent for our livelihood on the creativity and courage of the entrepreneurial men who accept the risks which generate our riches.

16. Most people are just plain stupid and need to be led by the hand and guided.

Bibliography

The following bibliography deals with the subject matter of this chapter.

John Buell and Tom De Luca	"Let's Start Talking About Socialism," *The Progressive*, March 1977.
John Patrick Diggins	"Why the Future Never Happened," *The New York Times Book Review*, October 20, 1985.
John B. Judis	"Socialism: Who Knows What It Is?" *In These Times*, January 23/29, 1985.
Robert Kuttner	*The Economic Illusion: False Choices Between Prosperity and Social Justice*. Boston, MA: Houghton Mifflin Company, 1984.
Sidney Lens	"Why Not Try Radicalism: Old Ideas for New Socialists," *The Nation*, April 6, 1985.
Michael Novak	"Economic Rights: The Servile State," *Catholicism in Crisis*, October 1985.
Alec Nove	"Feasible Socialism?" *Dissent*, Summer 1985.
James L. Payne	"When the Rich Get Richer," *Reason*, February 1984.
The People	"You've Heard the Lies About Socialism, Now Get the Facts," March 16, 1985.
Madsen Pirie	"Buying Out of Socialism," *Reason*, January 1986.
William Ryan	*Equality*. New York: Pantheon Books, 1981.
Robert J. Samuelson	"Escaping the Poverty Trap," *Newsweek*, September 10, 1984.
Ronald K. Shelp	"Entrepreneurship in the Information Society," *Vital Speeches of the Day*, August 15, 1985.
Time	"Socialism: Trials and Errors," March 13, 1978.
Michael Walzer	*Spheres of Justice: A Defense of Pluralism and Equality*. New York: Basic Books, Inc., 1983.

Index

affirmative action, 102-103
Aid to Families with Dependent
  Children (AFDC)
  as successful, 107-108
  as unsuccessful, 100, 104
Allen, Gary, 102
Americans for Democratic
  Action, 95
Aronowitz, Stanley, 142

Babeuf, Francois Noel
  (Gracchus), 27
Bellamy, Edward, 66
Bernstein, Eduard, 51, 56
blacks
  and poverty, 99
  women, 109
bourgeoisie
  vs. proletariat, 41-44
Buell, John, 138

capital
  in communes, 21
capitalism
  advantages of, 25-26, 146-147
  as undesirable, 60
  defined as property, 24-26
  destroys community, 141
  disadvantages of, 25-26,
    123-125
  evolving into socialism, 57-58,
    67-70
  myths of, 129-132
  oppresses workers, 124-126
children and poverty, 104
Christianity
  as religion of socialism, 32
class struggle, 43-44, 52, 56
  and economic relations, 58
  and free enterprise, 95
  origins of, 73
Cleveland, Grover, 87
Coe, Richard D., 106
Coleman, S., 123, 142
collectivism
  incompatible with human
    nature, 118
  strategies of, 95-97
Collum, Danny, 140

communes, 20-23
communism
  as oppressive, 25-26
Communist Manifesto, The, 52
community
  reflects socialist values, 140-
    141
Crum, Richard H., 118

De Leon, Daniel, 71
Drucker, Peter F., 137
Duncan, Greg J., 106

education, 103
  and the family, 103
  eliminating poverty, 92-93
  under socialism, 29
Engels, Friedrich, 72
entrepreneurs, 146-150
equality, 26-27
  and economic efficiency, 129-
    132
  under socialism, 28-30

Fabian Society, 59
family
  and welfare, 109-110
    as negative, 100-101
food stamps, 104, 107
Fourier, Charles, 20, 41
free enterprise, 104
  as ideal, 95, 146-150
  as just, 134-137

Galbraith, John Kenneth, 90, 132
George, Henry, 68
Gilder, George, 135, 145
Goldwater, Barry, 94
Gorz, Andre, 143
government, 95, 139
  aid during depression
    as beneficial, 83-85
    as harmful, 86-89
  as artificial, 72
  as tyrannical, 74
  programs for the poor
    as beneficial, 90-93, 106-
      110
    as harmful, 94-97, 98-105

Great Britain
  socialist party of, 95
Great Depression
  and government intervention
    as beneficial, 84-85
    as harmful, 87-89
Great Society program, 99, 107
Gutman, Herbert, 141

Hayek, Friedrich von, 97
Himmelfarb, Gertrude, 102
Hoover, Herbert C., 86
Hospers, John, 133

Indians, Native American
  as socialist community, 72-73
industrial system
  and class antagonism, 43
  evils of, 23

Johnson, Lyndon, 99

Kennedy, John F., 139
Keynesian economics, 132
Khrushchev, Nikita, 120
Kuttner, Robert, 128

Lassalle, Ferdinand, 37, 61
Lenin, N., 73
Luxemburg, Rosa, 55

Marx, Karl, 40, 72
  and *Das Kapital*, 62
  errors of, 61
  on capitalism, 124-125
  threat of, 95
McCrory, Gail, 108
Medicaid, 100
Morgan, Lewis Henry, 26, 72
Murray, Charles, 98, 107

nationalization, 95-96
Nietzsche, Friedrich, 122
Novak, Michael, 100

Owen, Robert, 35, 41, 61

Peterson, Dennis L., 120
Pierce, Charles S., 33
poverty
  and capitalism, 58
  and socialism, 38

and welfare
  alleviates, 89-93, 107-110,
    130
  contributes to, 104-105
  as unjust, 29
  attitudes toward, 99-100, 101,
    104-105
  causes of, 91, 135
  data on, 100
  reasons for, 91
  trends of, 99, 101-102, 104
  ways to eliminate, 34, 91-93
private enterprise system, 119-
  120
proletariat
  vs. bourgeoisie, 41-44
property
  and capitalism, 25
  belongs to everyone, 29
  private, 30, 95
  public, 143
Proudhon, Pierre Joseph, 24
  errors of, 41

Rich, Spencer, 110
Roosevelt, Franklin D., 83
Rousseau, Jean Jacques, 29
ruling class, 43
Ryan, William, 130

Saint-Simon, Claude Henri, 31,
  41, 61
Shaw, George Bernard, 61
Smyth, David, 116
socialism
  aberrations of, 41-44
  and Christianity, 31-34
  and the Church, 32-34, 140
  and Judaism, 33
  and production, 126-127
  and strikes, 64-65
  and the workers, 41-44
  economic growth
    as impossible, 134-137, 150
    as possible, 129-132
    as unimportant, 139-144
  equality of people, 28-30
  evolutionary
    as desirable, 37, 60-62, 67-
      70
    as impossible, 56-58
    as possible, 52-54

155